The Man Who Invented Hollywood

THE MAN WHO INVENTED HOLLYWOOD

The Autobiography of D. W. Griffith

A Memoir and Some Notes
edited and annotated
by James Hart
including the unfinished autobiography
of the film master

TOUCHSTONE PUBLISHING COMPANY
Louisville, Kentucky

FOR MY GRANDCHILDREN

JAY

GINA AND

JOHN

Foreword

"IT WAS HERE that I was born. Here also was whelped the wolf pup of want and hunger that was to shadow me all my life," writes D. W. Griffith in the pages of this book.

What seer could have foretold that, thirty-two years after that boy and his pup were born, on a certain fall day in 1907 there would be a dawning of utmost significance to the world of art and beauty. On that red-letter day, when the usually hungry, ex-Kentucky farm boy—lately an always-hungry itinerant actor and playwright—walked into Biograph's moving picture studio in New York and laid an armful of scenarios on film director Walter McCutcheon's desk (at the going price of $5 each, if used), Creation stirred and began the happy incubation of a new child in its womb.

For tall, restless, hook-nosed David Wark Griffith, known in gimcrack theatres as Lawrence Griffith, walking into a despised movie studio was an actor's nadir of degradation. Traditional thespians from stars to spear-holders held the peep show "flickers" in utmost contempt. But "wolf pup" was no respecter of traditions.

"Please read my scenarios," said Griffith haughtily to director McCutcheon. Then, adding that he might also condescend to lend his great acting talents to Biograph,

Griffith left with empty hope and emptier stomach. Never in his wildest dreams could he have imagined that he had taken his first step in the creating of a new, vital, and utterly original art form, possibly the greatest of art forms—one which was to use older classic arts as tools—the motion picture!

Film art was to be the first new art created by man since the Greeks had formalized the theatre twenty-five centuries earlier with the tragedies of Aeschylus and the Attic Comedies of Aristophanes.

The creation of a new art form is a long leap forward in human advancement. Either it grafts a significant limb on the body of contemporary cultures or it elevates us into new cultures, new truths of the heart, new enrichments. There is ample reason to believe that the modern film is effecting cultural changes that drastically modify the patterns of our human behavior.

When Griffith first picked up his megaphone in 1907, the novelty of the "galloping flicks" was petering out. Scorned and damned by professional artists as a claptrap fad on the flea circus level, film flickered ever feebler in amusement parlors and circus sideshows—but never in theatres. When Mr. Griffith hung up his megaphone in 1931, he had elevated the lowly film to the most pervasive, dynamic art form in motion picture critic, Frank Woods. It was *The Clansman* by Thomas Dixon.

Evolutionary changes are not always slow adaptations to environment. At times evolution leaps mysteriously forward in sudden, abrupt, and drastic mutations. Thus it was with *The Birth of a Nation*, hailed by many as the first and greatest motion picture classic ever made.

The Birth of a Nation, as *The Clansman* was finally called, was a twelve-reel film with a musical score! Who had ever heard of anything like it? Who would show it? The few who had seen it were dumbfounded. After a private showing President Wilson gasped that it was "like writing history with lightning!"

When the most important film ever made was shown in New York's Liberty Theatre (at $2 admission fee), the public was overwhelmed. Why should a succession of mere photographs provoke such excitement, such emotion? Why indeed! Because discovering a new art form is an adventure as memorable as discovering a new planet. *The Birth of a Nation* told a wondrous story in a new and wondrous way. Unbelievers at last became believers. A new art form had been created. Film. And its creator was D. W. Griffith.

But the first truly "one-man" classic did not just happen. It was fashioned with blood, sweat, and the Promethean stubbornness of Griffith. "His struggles," as Terry Ramsaye puts it in his *A Million and One Nights*, "are reminiscent of Bernard Palissey, the 16th Century French enameler, burning his home to keep the fires of his furnace going."

Griffith didn't have any furniture to burn, but he did have friends and crews to gouge, and even cadged a few dollars—or a few pennies—from strangers. Such pennies paid off in dollars. *The Birth of a Nation* cost $100,000, but it took in $18,000,000 in just a few years! And as the only film of that period that can enthrall audiences of today, it is *still* making money!

But the very success of Griffith's *The Birth of a Nation*—and his next spectacular, *Intolerance*—carried the seeds of destruction for the "one man, one film" idea. Lavish theatres were needed to exhibit such lavish films. In turn, lavish theatres became Frankenstein's monsters with a voracious appetite for more films to keep them open. Enter the great pioneer builders—Laemmle, Fox, Zukor, Loew, Kent, the Schencks, the Warners, the Balabans—who skyrocketed the nickelodeons into production-distribution-exhibition chains worth billions of dollars. Griffith's "one man, one film" art form exploded into worldwide industrial empires that manufactured a strange product: motion pictures.

A corporation's goal is efficiency—a beautifully oiled, cybernetic enterprise turning out the predictable products demanded by the sales department. But any self-respecting cybernetic system would go bananas if it were asked to manufacture products of an *unpredictable art form*, no two of them alike in size, cost, or content. Early pioneer promoters did not think of films as a new art form but as artsy-craftsy novelties to be sold by the yard. So it was a natural step for the new corporations to industrialize film production in order to guarantee their thousands of theatres a steady flow of "product." Out went the "one man, one film" system; in came the assembly-line production. Out went quality; in came quantity. Art was shoved into the back seat; industry took over the steering wheel. Out went Griffith, the individualist; in came corporate chains of command. The art form became a billion-dollar industry.

But the Promethean in Griffith the artist would not die. He fought vigorously against the assembly-line moguls who thought film could be bottled and sold like soda pop; who ganged up to destroy the quixotic "one man, one film" notion. Defying them all, D.W. borrowed money wherever he could and continued to make films his own way: no written scripts, no budgets, and no fixed schedules. He managed to make one more successful classic film, *Broken Blossoms*. But on most other films he lost money. The Establishment snickered and dumped him as an expensive liability.

Griffith's gamut ran from saga to poetry. Scott Fitzgerald's giddy new postwar world of bathtub gin, jazz, sex, and silk step-ins was not D.W.'s bag. The Griffith star was setting. Conversely, the star of one of his pupils (C. B. DeMille) began to rise when he flamboyantly exploited sex, religion, and bathtubs.

Beaten, frustrated, and deeply in debt (he owed two million dollars) Griffith finally agreed to join the Establishment and work for Adolph Zukor as a hired hand. He made three films, all pale copies of DeMille's bespangled spectaculars. Griffith was let out. Hollywood said "get lost!" D.W. got lost.

Sound came. Griffith was still lost. But in 1931 he rented an old New York studio, hired some actors, and made *The Struggle*. It was his last film and—final irony—his worst film. Audiences laughed at it. The Great Master faded into the oblivion of cheap hotels and cheaper bars.

In 1936 I had a brainstorm. As president of the Motion Picture Academy I was in dire need of a drawing card for a faltering Academy Award Banquet. Of course! The Master. Where was he? Nobody knew. I tracked him down in Kentucky. Would Mr. Griffith come to Hollywood to accept a special Oscar "for his outstanding contributions to the art of the film?" He would. The applause was deafening and sincere when he stepped up to receive his Special Award. His presence made the Academy Banquet. For one day he was headline news. Then he became yesterday's news, which in Hollywood means no news. He dropped out of sight again.

In 1939 the Screen Directors Guild again tracked him down and talked D.W. into surfacing from oblivion long enough to accept a Life Membership at the Directors Guild annual banquet. In his honor the Guild also inaugurated its most prestigious tribute, the D. W. Griffith Award, to be bestowed (when merited) on directors who, in their lifetime, have "made outstanding contributions to the art of filmmaking."

At that same time I invited Mr. and Mrs. Griffith (a new young wife) to visit the *Mr. Smith Goes to Washington* set and watch us shoot a scene. I am not easily cowed. But when I began rehearsing a scene with the god of all directors looking over my shoulder, an acute attack of stage-fright hit me. My quivering voice, shaking knees, and sweating palms said it loud and clear: "Bow down, boy. You're in the presence of the Great One!"

D.W. went into seclusion again at the Knickerbocker Hotel. At night he roamed the streets of Hollywood unrecognized and forgotten in the city that was built on the pillars of his art.

On July 23, 1948, D. W. Griffith died of a cerebral hemorrhage.

In eulogizing D.W., old friend Donald Crisp, acting president of the Motion Picture Academy, said: ". . . It is hard to believe that the industry could not have found use for his great talent." And from Charles Brackett, vice-president of the Academy: "there was no solution for Griffith but a kind of frenzied beating on the barred doors of one day after another. . . . He lies here, the embittered years forgotten—David Wark Griffith—the Great."

And there were written tributes. Lionel Barrymore wrote: "[He] is dead and there is wailing and gnashing of teeth. Yes, but a trifle belatedly." From Frank Capra: "Since Griffith there has been no major improvement in the art of film direction." And from C. B. DeMille: "People used to flatter me by saying that D. W. Griffith and I were rivals. Griffith had no rivals. He was the teacher of us all."

And when the Master was buried in a small unmarked grave in Mt. Tabor Cemetery in his home town in Kentucky, the Muses wept as they heard the echo of his own words: "We tinkered daily with the movie toy, like children making up games. . . . There finally came a day, however, when nobody cried 'Eureka!' any more . . . and there was a great stillness. The front office had won."

David Wark Griffith, one of the great names in American film history, was fated to be forgotten by the great industry his art had proliferated, forgotten because he was a loner, a rebel, a proud Titan. But no one can ever again create a film art. That honor belongs solely to the Master. And all the corporation heads and all their assembly-lines could not kill Griffith's "one man, one film" concept of artistic filmmaking. His concept took root again in my small studio on Poverty Row, in the late 20's. Its seed was so fertile that the concept spread, and grew, and finally flowered in the Golden Age of Movies in the 30's and 40's.

That Golden Age was Hollywood's real monument to David Wark Griffith. And every great picture made today adds yet another wreath to that memorial.

August 29, 1971   —Frank Capra

Introduction

DESPITE the time-to-time nudging of various literary advisers to cut, edit, or rewrite the autobiography of D. W. Griffith, I have taken the gambit of presenting within the following pages the original rough draft manuscript of Griffith's life (the only literary effort definitely known to be in his own words) from his childhood to and including *The Birth of a Nation*, unabridged and unedited except for spelling and punctuation, solely that the reader may judge for himself the limitations of D. W. Griffith as a thinking and feeling man and why—with narrow story values chained to exploding techniques—he could rise no higher than he did. It is hoped that the narrative of supplementary notes brings into equal perspective the incredible capabilities of this greatest of all motion picture directors.

The circumstances surrounding the writing of the autobiography of D. W. Griffith are described elsewhere in this book. Regarding the monograph of supplementary notes, however, there were in my possession more than 600 pages of longhand notes from the Griffith interviews when my *Liberty* magazine story was published in 1939, propelling the old director back to Hollywood again. These notes were originally destined for the "fleshing-out" of the first draft of the Griffith manuscript—for detail, description, anecdote, definition, direction, etc. Several well-known Louisville newsmen, who had sat in on some of the Griffith interviews in the old Brown Hotel lobby from time to time, urged me to finish the book as a biography. My New York agent, Mrs. Ruth Aley of Maxwell Aley Associates, also opted for incorporating the notes, which contain much material that have never been published before, into the Griffith manuscript as a first draft for submission to a New York publisher. (The working title of this early effort was *The Man Who Invented Hollywood*.) World War II was at hand, however, and D. W. Griffith was again out of step with the times, so the manuscript of notes and dictation gathered dust for thirty-two years.

Although the autobiography of D. W. Griffith is, of course, an unfinished work, it is presented here in its initial form as it was dictated by Griffith himself and reveals more of the workings of the director's mind than any brief the writer could devise. If the Griffith buff, researcher and student, can look past the Victorian shadings to the eternal verities he sought (and also look past the mindless Dorian Gray decline to the monument he left behind) the real meaning of Griffith and his work may take shape.

As noted elsewhere in these pages, this is not a definitive work and therefore no bibliography is appended. Although I am conversant with most if not all of the important writings on the life and career of D. W. Griffith from Eisenstein to MacGowan, including the curious contributions of Linda Arvidson and Homer Croy, a bibliography was considered superfluous since such material is rather easily obtainable and, after all, we had the man himself at first hand.

Griffith's films within the past two decades have become required study in courses on the art of the motion picture in many universities, and the current rise of Griffith film festivals across the land hopefully indicates a renascence of D. W. Griffith and his works. But the bibliography extant on the great director himself is still largely a wasteland insofar as Griffith's character, insight, and motivation are concerned. In the last half-century, for instance, a small but confusing catalogue of so-called Griffith portraits have emerged, ranging from the pen-and-ink of a St. Francis of Assisi to the fading daguerreotype of a mere instinctive genius. That some gray areas may be sketched in on all these starkly black-and-white vignettes is the end purpose of this cameo exercise on the film poet from Centerfield, Kentucky.

James Hart
Louisville, Kentucky
June 12, 1971

Contents

The Man Who Invented Hollywood

A Memoir

MUCH LIKE Melville's Ishmael, who got to sea whenever there was "a damp, drizzly November" in his soul, D. W. Griffith betimes fled Hollywood for the catharsis of his old Kentucky home. Indeed, each time his career bottomed out, there were few Louisville newspapermen in the '20s and '30s who didn't know that shortly the film master could be found under his famous old straw hat, sitting in a rocker on the side porch of his sister's white frame house in LaGrange, Kentucky, a small town in Oldham County, some twenty miles from Louisville. There he would spend his mornings playing the country squire, waving to acquaintances and reading Dickens and Whitman, until he tired of the game and would have Dick Reynolds, his black chauffeur and old family friend, drive him in his Mercedes to Louisville, where the director maintained a suite in the Brown Hotel. After all, most of his boyhood friends were dead, and Oldham County was dry.

My study of D. W. Griffith began with just such a sketch, to be fleshed and toned by later visits. It was a long sitting—off and on from 1932 to 1940. D. W. Griffith, a complex man full of paradoxes, was many things to many people. There is no one who can claim to have been continuously and intimately associated with the great director throughout his life; therefore, any portrait of this flawed genius must be necessarily lacking in depth and definition. To his family, for instance, he was devoted and generous; to Lillian Gish, Cecil B. DeMille, Frank Capra, and many others who rose to stardom, he was "teacher to us all"; yet to the press he was arrogant and evasive; and at least to some oldsters in his home county, he was never more than "Colonel Jake's boy" or "that Hollywood fellow." Again, he was scrupulously honest about paying his debts but freely admitted to stealing stories and lines from well-known authors. He gave away thousands of dollars but seldom carried money on his person and expected others to pick up the tab. And there were many easy generalizations. He has often, for instance, been characterized as "alone and tragic." The tragedy was real enough, but if he was alone, it was because he wanted it that way. So any picture of D. W. Griffith depended largely upon who you were and where you were and the particular season of his career. Nevertheless, despite this plus and minus catalogue, we had some exciting and exhilarating sessions on the old side porch in LaGrange, Kentucky. Looking back, it appears that D. W. Griffith revealed more of himself in decline than at any other period in his life.

One day in 1933 an International News dispatch reported that D. W. Griffith had been "kissed out" of Hollywood again. World-famous for his *The Birth of a Nation*, he had made almost five hundred motion pictures and had been named director of the year in 1931 by the Academy of Motion Picture Arts and Sciences. The following year, however, he made *The Struggle*, his worst picture, and by 1933 could not get bankrolled or hired in the motion picture industry. It was an old feud. The producers had once more categorized D. W. Griffith as a muralist whose paintings ran off the wall, and the director had retorted again that Hollywood was becoming a medium of finance, not art. My city editor on the old *Louisville Herald-Post*, Bland Ballard, waited two weeks, then confidently sent me to LaGrange to ask D. W. Griffith about his plans for the future.

The old man was sitting in the rocker. He was sullen and suspicious and barked that Boyd Martin, the drama critic for the *Louisville Courier-Journal*, "had phoned for an appointment"—an oblique reference to my uninvited presence. After a bit of skirmishing, he thawed and confided that he was more interested in hearing from someone who could fix the plumbing in his sister's bathroom. (This anecdote has been mauled in print several times.)

The interview seemed to be off the pad as he grinned and exhibited a new fedora, pulling the brim down on one side, and asked if the hat obscured his nose, adding quite candidly that he considered himself ugly; but perhaps he was only fishing. At any rate, his nose was indeed large and hooked in the bargain—a truly Olympian promontory—although I thought him not ugly at all but possessed of a rather rugged and striking face, not unlike those that float out of a Bronte novel. Curiously enough, although he was five feet ten and about one hundred sixty-five pounds, he seemed much larger and taller, perhaps due to his erect carriage and military step. After an hour or so of small talk, mostly about Centerfield, his home village five miles away, he rose, said something about a plumber, and entered the house. Only then did it occur to

me that he had not answered any of my questions about his plans in the motion picture industry.

One week later, another INS dispatch, this one datelined New York, had D. W. Griffith sailing for Europe to interest foreign capital in a motion picture alliance.

Griffith returned briefly to LaGrange in 1934 for the funeral of his sister, Ruth. The European trip had been fruitless. A year later he surfaced again in LaGrange. This time, quite by chance, I was the only reporter aware of his return. He asked me to sit on the story, promising a better one later. (He kept his word.) Then he told me that he had visited Ballard Clark, a LaGrange attorney; had presented him with a heavy silver cigarette case as a token of their long friendship; and had asked the lawyer to file suit for divorce from Linda Arvidson, whom Griffith had not seen for twenty-six years. (LaGrange had been Griffith's legal residence for many years.) He explained that Miss Arvidson's lawyers had trailed him across Europe, dunning him for maintenance payments, and he wanted this particular chase over with, regardless of what Oldham County thought about divorce and the mores of Hollywood.

A few nights later, however, Griffith appeared in the Greyhound, a large gambling casino across the river from Louisville, flanked by two chorus girls from the Gayety Theater, a Louisville burlesque house. He took a ringside table, ordered champagne, then recognized me and waved happily. I was writing a show business and gossip column at the time and asked him if he thought it was wise to appear in public. Griffith winked and assured me that it was a maneuver to hoodwink the press as to his real purpose in Louisville. An odd gambit.

The next morning he was back sitting in the old rocker in LaGrange, reading Dickens. Since he had already appeared in public, I informed Francis "Jeff" Wylie, my colleague and editor of our magazine section, that Griffith was back. Wylie went out to LaGrange and got a good story, reporting that he had found Griffith in an expansive mood and quite willing to talk about Hollywood. Jeff Wylie was an excellent reporter (he later became editor of *Time* magazine's Boston Bureau) and was an Englishman to boot, and D. W. Griffith thought God was an Englishman.

Shortly afterward, Griffith submerged for another year, then was seen in a small street-side bar operated by the famous Seelbach Hotel. I went to see him at the Brown Hotel, and he told me, quite as if he were reading a grocery list, that he was marrying a Miss Evelyn Baldwin the following Saturday evening. He had, after all, been right about hoodwinking the press and enjoyed the joke. He said casually that the bride, who would be accompanied by her mother, was from Long Island and was the daughter of an old friend who had been lost at sea. (Later I learned that Miss Baldwin, although not an actress, had been given a small part in Griffith's last picture, *The Struggle*, and that they had met for the first time at a tea in New York when Miss Baldwin was thirteen. Upon being introduced, Griffith was reputed to have exclaimed, "You are Little Nell!")

On the nuptial evening, Griffith told Billy Nast, the maitre d'hotel, to prepare a wedding breakfast for fifty guests. An hour later he cut the list to ten. The minister was late, then the groom disappeared. Jack Thompson, a *Louisville Times* reporter, found him in the Bluegrass Room bar downstairs and returned the director to the wedding party, albeit Griffith was quite sober and seemed years younger. So at eight P.M., March 2, 1936, D. W. Griffith was married in a salon on the mezzanine floor of the Brown Hotel. Griffith, 62, was reading Arthur Brisbane and Bernarr Macfadden then and believed that he could live

140 years "if he watched himself." The new Mrs. Griffith was charming, attractive, and shy—the classic Griffith heroine—and 22 years old.

After a honeymoon in Florida and a quick trip to Hollywood to accept an award for his contributions to the film industry, Griffith and his bride were reported traveling in the East. In 1938, the couple returned to LaGrange.

About this time, the late Fulton Oursler, then editor of *Liberty* magazine, missed a train; a newspaper went on strike; and D. W. Griffith got another chance at Hollywood. I was then a bylined feature writer for the *Chicago Evening American* and doing syndicate material for International News Service. Between trains on his way to New York, Oursler phoned Harry Reutlinger, my city editor, and asked him to lunch. Oursler, who liked to talk about the movies, was a great admirer of D. W. Griffith, and when Reutlinger mentioned my Griffith relationship, he elected to miss a train in order to accompany the city editor to the *American* and ask me to do a story on D. W. Griffith "and what's wrong with Hollywood." Other commitments deterred me at the time, but shortly afterward the newly formed newspaper guild went on strike, and I was "at liberty" in Louisville.

In LaGrange, Griffith received the idea of a *Liberty* magazine article with great enthusiasm. He began declaiming about the block system of merchandising movies (forcing upon the exhibitor two or more pictures as a package deal), the evils of continuous performance, et cetera. He also liked the name *Liberty*, reminding me that *The Birth of a Nation* was first shown in New York, in the old Liberty Theater. It was a good omen for the old man; the lackluster look was gone and for a few moments he seemed younger, spilling out the words in a great rush. (His favorite word when elated was "wonderful.") We had several such ses-

5

sions in LaGrange and in the Brown Hotel, and then one day I showed him a letter from Oscar Graeve, assistant editor of *Liberty*, accepting the article (See Appendix I) under the byline of D. W. Griffith. (I had ghostwritten many such articles, but this one was special. It was my hope that the right sort of publicity would boost D. W. Griffith back over the fence to where he belonged.) Griffith was ecstatic. He windmilled his arms and shouted that we would do great things together or something like that, and began outlining one magazine story idea after another. For a moment, I thought he had gone mad.

While composing the magazine article, Griffith had dictated many voluminous and discursive notes. He now referred diffidently to this pile of memoranda and offhandedly suggested that his life story might be in order. No sooner had I agreed than he immediately launched into a filibuster on guide lines. He disliked desks; we would work in surroundings "that evoke creation," meaning outdoors. Another thing. He didn't like the sight of pencil and paper, so I would simply have to remember all he said. As it turned out, we would take to the side porch for each session or tool around to nearby Cox's Lake for a swim and then lie on the grass while Griffith chain smoked cigarettes and reached back into his childhood and the early movies. He was repetitive and insisted upon going over and over a particular event until it was firmly fixed in his mind—and mine. He was proud of his figure and liked to pose in swim shorts before the nubile country lasses, sometimes doing calisthenics on the diving board. Whenever he emerged from the lake, however, he always dressed immediately, observing that he was subject to colds and influenza. He carried pills in each pocket. Sometimes our sessions took place in the Brown. After each such story conference, however, I would stay behind after

Griffith left, scribbling hastily and racking my mind for every scrap of Griffith memorabilia. I met his wife only once or twice in all those months, and then briefly; however, my impression is that he was a happily married man or was giving a good imitation of one.

One day he failed to keep an appointment in Louisville, and I learned later that he had called Jack Thompson, the *Times* reporter, and that the two had hightailed out like Schneider's cat for every small and out-of-the-way bistro from The Little Rascal in the black belt to Steve's Place on the levee. D. W. Griffith disliked the press as a body, particularly drama critics, but Thompson was his boon companion on such junkets, perhaps because the police reporter was discreet, cared little about Hollywood or LaGrange, and had the political connections to keep Griffith out of trouble. In addition, Thompson had a great admiration for the old film master and would listen to him, glass in hand, for hours. Griffith once remarked that Jack Barrymore had his bulldog; he had Thompson. (Barrymore was noted for taking his old bulldog into speakeasies during the prohibition era.)

In general, however, Griffith was sober and reliable in those days and in full possession of his faculties, and the drinking bout with the police reporter—there having been only one or two such lapses I can remember —should be considered as only the circumstances and not the man himself, at least not at this time.

The other incident grew out of a remark Griffith made while reading a column by Arthur Brisbane. He said quite suddenly that he would like to become a columnist and asked if I knew any syndicate people. My impression then was that he wanted to write about Hollywood. King Features, McNaught, McClure Syndicate, NEA, and Associated Features were canvassed and the replies were all favorable, the last named appearing to be the best. When Bob Farrell, the Associated Features representative, arrived at the Brown, however, Griffith failed to keep his appointment. Thompson finally ran him aground in the Seelbach bar down the street and towed him back to the hotel, where Griffith announced to the waiting feature salesman that he wished to write a column similar to Brisbane's. "I want to write on world affairs," he said defiantly, and no one could budge him from this stand.

"We can get to that later, perhaps," cajoled Farrell, "but right now, Mr. Griffith, our papers would be interested in you only because of your Hollywood connections."

"Brisbane."

So the syndicate man went away, and D. W. Griffith returned to his bar.

Griffith was not an easy subject despite his initial élan and exuberance. He insisted, for instance, that I write the script (his autobiography) in "his style," yet he could offer no samples of his writing. None of his silent movie scripts had been put on paper, and apparently he had no valid claim to anything in print under his own name. When Linda Arvidson caught up with him in court over alimony payments, she testified under oath that she alone had written *The Wild Duck*, a poem published by Leslie's *Weekly*, and a play entitled *A Fool and a Girl*. Griffith had claimed authorship of both. (He confided to me, as he did to several other reporters, that he had always wanted to be a writer rather than a director.)

Often he was arbitrarily vague and gave little evidence of the prodigious memory credited to him. It is said that Napoleon, when displeased by questions relating to this or that battle strategy, would switch the talk to vintage brandy. Something of this sort transpired with Griffith, and on such occasions the interviews disintegrated into summer smoke whenever the story line

ran counter to the image he was trying to project. Yet there were other days when he was distressingly frank to the last detail, such as his experiences in a country school or his mounting despair during the making of *The Birth of a Nation* or his ego-rending association with Zukor at Paramount.

Gradually I began to realize that he was not dictating pages, but was rehearsing and directing scenes out of his past. If the "scene" didn't fit, he would alter it or delete it. Sometimes, when the manuscript read like *True Heart Susie* or the *Adventures of Frank Merriwell*, he could be induced to do it over; but generally my role was that of "cutter," smoothing syntax and grammar and editing countless "retakes." He would have a small tantrum over the deletion of a single pet cliché or prosy sentence. Once when he thought he had injured my feelings, however, he quickly digressed into an amusing story and laughed uproariously. He was a thoroughly sensitive man. On one such occasion he told me slyly that Lillian Gish had been the only woman in his life for many years, but that he thought too much of her to marry her, then chuckled and added quickly that he couldn't allow any such allusion in the manuscript. Another time, he said he had fallen in love with Lady Diana Manners—"the most beautiful woman in the world and the daughter of a hundred earls," but that he couldn't wear striped pants all his life, and besides, she was married. That, too, was penciled out. He was always the actor, and I never knew which hat he would be wearing, but he consistently maintained an aloof, reserved manner, almost courtly. No one ever called him Dave. He was not modest, alternating between arrogance and humility, but withal was a remarkable man: one well worth listening to.

The working title of the autobiography was *D. W. Griffith and the Wolf*. He said that poverty and he were old friends. It is a

7

cloyed, sentimental tale; episodic and evasive; yet it is the only source material extant, except for his notes, that describe his early life and the making of *The Birth of a Nation* in his own words. The errors inherent in the work are discussed later in this book, but none of his little fictions was malicious and some of them he actually believed to be the truth.

It should be noted, too, that throughout the writing of his autobiography he never allowed a disparaging statement about any individual to find its way into the manuscript.

On June 17, 1939, *Liberty* magazine published the story I wrote for D. W. Griffith. The next day Hal Roach, producer of Hal Roach Studios, wired Griffith, congratulating his former boss on the story and asking him to return to Hollywood to assist in producing and directing *One Million B.C.* The old director had his second chance. He was wildly elated. He would see Capra and talk about the new trend in pictures. He yelled something about his horoscope being in conjunction with the stars and packed his bags, taking a carbon copy of the unfinished autobiography with him, promising to return soon, "and we'll finish this thing in style." His horoscope was wrong, and the signed original copy of this manuscript lay on my closet shelf for thirty-two years.

Soon after World War II, a cult of the early motion picture arose, particularly on the campuses of the large universities. To these film students the pictures of the '20s and '30s appeared one-dimensional and involved with dated fashions. Then they discovered D. W. Griffith's films, and the humanity and eloquence of the man himself emerged. The renascense of D. W. Griffith began. They learned that D. W. Griffith was involved with style, that quality which gives excellence to any art and never changes. The fashions of his times and the conventional ways of society, which take new forms almost weekly and particularly so in the '20s and '30s, never concerned him. Like Faulkner, he was interested only in the eternal verities. Sherwood Anderson had a fired genius for capturing life in a series of moments, and so did D. W. Griffith on the screen. Like Anderson, too, he was episodic, but so was Dickens and many other great writers. Today's students are fortunate in that they do not judge these films by the standards of fifty years ago, a luxury made possible simply because time itself has dialed the proper perspective.

With the end of the World War I, for instance, the American public turned to realism. Sherwood Anderson, Theodore Dreiser, Sinclair Lewis, Ernest Hemingway, John Dos Passos, and F. Scott Fitzgerald, among others, upset the old idols; and the film critics and producers mounted a witch hunt of their own for anything that smacked of Victorian taste. In their zeal and myopia, D. W. Griffith was put to the stake. Time became his ally, however, and today his pictures are viewed again with enthusiasm, but this time in sharper focus. Also, in the same sense, it may be said that the faults of Griffith's pictures are the faults of his autobiography, too—Victorian morality; prosy language; sentimentality; but all belonging now, happily enough, to the euphemisms and romanticism of the past. And his autobiography, too, should be viewed from this same platform.

If the moviegoer finds that because of these passages he can view the modern motion picture with greater enjoyment and clarity, knowing that this is his art, too, then our debt to D. W. Griffith is discharged. After all, that's everything Griffith wanted: to make the public see.

Balked at the Altar; released August 1908.

Marion Leonard and Mary Pickford;
The Lonely Villa, June 1909.

Griffith heightened suspense by cross cutting scenes
in this film; *The Lonely Villa,* June 1909.

An ad for two Biograph films. Griffith directed *The Redman's View*, one of almost 150 flicks that he cranked out in 1909.

One of Mary Pickford's first films with Biograph and D. W. Griffith; *Her First Biscuit*, June 1909.

The only known photograph of D. W. Griffith's father, Colonel Jacob Wark Griffith.

From the beginning, Griffith was fascinated by the story of the Civil War;
In Old Kentucky, September 1909.

An ingenious and, at that time,
innovative use of lighting;
Gertrude Robinson;
Pippa Passes, October 1909.

Watercolor of Flexner & Staadecker's bookstore, which D.W. called his "university."

America's Sweetheart and the public's favorite Biograph Girl, Mary Pickford; *The Englishman and the Girl,* February 1910.

Griffith used both close-up shots to show nuances of expression (as here with Mary Pickford) and very long shots in *Ramona;* May 1910.

California provided a wealth of on-location sites; *Ramona*, May 1910.

The young D. W. Griffith. During his Biograph years, he took films from the limitations of the stage and created a new art form.

This two-reel Civil War film was released in two parts—Biograph was not ready to break away from the old, one-reel film concept; *His Trust*, January 1911.

Originally called The *Primitive Man,* this film used special effects; *Man's Genesis,* July 1911.

The Primitive Man or *Man's Genesis* was billed as a "psychological comedy" by Griffith and Biograph; July 1911.

This film was an early forerunner of Hal Roach's *One Million B.C.,* portions of which were directed by Griffith; *Man's Genesis,* July 1911.

"THE NEW YORK HAT"

THE CHURCH
BOARD INVESTIGATES

The New York Hat, starring Mary Pickford
and Lionel Barrymore, illustrates Griffith's
good use of character actors.
When the church board started to investigate,
the viewer knew Mary Pickford
would be in trouble;
The New York Hat, December 1912.

The Hollywood
Gold Rush

by D. W. Griffith

D.K

D. W. Griffith

"THE HOLLYWOOD GOLD RUSH"

~~or~~ *by*

"D. W. Griffith ~~and the Wolf~~"

as told to Jim Hart

Prologue

A scant half century ago Queen Victoria was
firmly seated on the throne of Great Britian and the
world slid along nicely at three miles an hour.

Down in Old Kentucky, near Louisville, was
the house of my father, Colonel Jacob Wark Griffith, a
Confederate cavalry officer. The house was on a small
hill and on all sides sloped meadows where sheep and
cows and horses often grazed. Beyond a field in front
of the house ran a dusty turnpike that had been laid by
my father.

Once there had been quite a pretentious place--
more or less like the popular conception of Kentucky
mansions-- with poplar and osage orange groves leading
up to its portals. Gerillas disguised as union raiders, *burned the*

Prologue

A SCANT half-century ago Queen Victoria was firmly seated on the throne of Great Britain and the world slid along nicely at three miles an hour.

Down in Old Kentucky, near Louisville, was the house of my father, Colonel Jacob Wark Griffith, a Confederate cavalry officer. The house was on a small hill and on all sides sloped meadows where sheep and cows and horses often grazed. Beyond a field in front of the house ran a dusty turnpike that had been laid by my father.

Once there had been quite a pretentious place—more or less like the popular conception of Kentucky mansions—with poplar and osage orange groves leading up to its portals. Guerrillas, disguised as union raiders, burned the house in the first year of the war. This second house that father built was quite small. And it was here that I was born. Here also was whelped the wolf pup of want and hunger that was to shadow me all my life.

A narrow lane led from our house to the turnpike. Sometimes by day along this old pike moved droves of cattle, white splashes of sheep, rattling carts and wagons, jogging buggies. By night these same buggies carried sweethearts and the flapping leather covers were often gilded by the new white spring moon.

None of my wildest boyhood dreams dared to picture Old Lady Luck boosting me down that turnpike into a future generously salted with great names, shoals of beautiful women, Presidents, prime ministers . . . royalty. All wined and dined the farmer boy from Kentucky. Well—I hear you—maybe they weren't full course dinners, *but I got snacks out of them, anyway.*

One of these snacks was donated by Mr. David Lloyd George. It was in the spring of 1917 on the terrace of famed No. 10 Downing Street. From the table where the prime minister and I were at breakfast, we could see through a window into the council chamber of Parliament. On one wall of this room hung a great map profusely dotted with tiny pegs showing the exact position of the Allied forces on the Western Front.

Here were gathered the bigwigs of the British War Department for a conference with Lloyd George. The conference was set for ten o'clock. The fate of the British empire, or for that matter, the whole world, hung in balance. We were still at breakfast and it was but a few minutes before ten. A brilliant conversationalist, Lloyd George kept talking several minutes after the conference deadline, while I hung on his every word and nervously eyed the pegs on the great map.

Mr. Bonar Law, who succeeded Lloyd George as prime minister, greatly reminded me of our own Calvin Coolidge. Both were extremely tight lipped. Yet both, among their intimates or unimportant visitors like myself, could get off a salty wisecrack with the best of them. His chief relaxation was to gather a group around the piano in the evening at weekend parties and sing Scotch hymns. Lord Beaverbrook's country place at Leatherhead in Surrey often resounded to them.

Another snack came from President Warren Harding who was one of the jolliest good fellows ever to live in the White House. Once, when holding a White House reception, he let me sit in the President's chair. While I tingled in the President's chair he stood near a great window and shook hands with the visitors as they filed through the room. One dear old lady—evidently confused by the great event of shaking hands with the President of the United States—bustled out of line and headed for me. "Oh, Mr. President!" she squeaked. Boy! What a boot I got out of that! Yes, she wore bifocals. President Harding, you know, was a handsome man.

Another memorable snack found me with the President, Mrs. Harding, and the Ned McLeans one night. We men adjourned after dinner to a poker game. This constituted the President's favorite recreation. And the particular brand of poker he played was called "Ferguson." Although I was no stranger to good old stud or draw poker, this Ferguson game had me hexed. For the uninitiated, it represented the quickest way to lose your shirt that I ever encountered. Sitting in the game with President Harding and me were Charlie Dawes and several other tycoons so wealthy that the disreputable old wolf that had been trailing me ever since I left my Kentucky village got the ague. As the game progressed, however, I soon heard Friend Wolf sniffing at my elbow. After attempting to make a three-card draw look like a pat hand, I was being rapidly towed Over the Hill to the Poorhouse when President Harding, now out of the game, leaned over my shoulder, began playing my hands, and soon had me out of hock. Can you imagine a President of the United States being human enough to do this for a common motion picture person?

On several occasions, I had fireside chats with that tragic idealist, Woodrow Wilson, when he was President. As I remember it, however, he never offered me so much as a single hot dog.

Even without the hot dog, however, mine has been, I believe, not an empty life.

Part One

THE IRIS OPENS on my old Kentucky home, twenty miles from Louisville. Life in Louisville was not tame in my youth. There were concerts, dramatic performances, vaudeville, beer gardens, open gambling, and "hot spots"—too hot for this circumspect day. Not infrequently, Barnum & Bailey's circus would calliope in, followed by Dwight L. Moody, evangelist, fervently shouting sinners to their knees.

In the country, however, entertainment consisted mostly of listening to whittling oldsters by the horse trough before the general store fight the Civil War over again—with ever-increasing victories; reading Leslie's *Weekly* by a kerosene lamp; listening to the old sentimental vocal and piano music in the parlor where gathered our sisters' beaux. Picnics, ice cream socials, camp meetings, and county fairs were events.

Now and then, of course, a couple good neighbors would flare into open argument, after which one or more would be gathered up, their value as live citizens completely nil. Then the community at large would be treated to the unmatched drama of a Kentucky murder trial in the old gray courthouse. In our section, however, there were no feudists in the strict sense of the word. I rather think that the liquidated citizen or citizens was/were merely the victim of sheer boredom.

Make no mistake, I hold no nostalgic grief for the past. Edison, Ford, and Marconi were still dreams back in those days . . . so were the plumbers.

My father and grandfather would seem similar to the roving Yancey in Edna Ferber's grand novel, *Cimarron*. Adventure was meat, drink, and all to these three. To this day, whenever some kind but deluded soul mentions my motion picture career, suggesting that it must have been extremely adventurous and exciting to have been midwife at the birth of a new industry, etc., the long shadows of these knights fall across my path . . . and immediately my career appears about as thrilling and adventurous as that of a woolly-faced lamb in a Blue Grass pasture.

The family legend as related by my Scotch-grained mother, whom I had never known to trouble to lie about anything, begins some time before the American Revolution with England's tranquillity wearing on great-great-grandfather's nerves. This Griffith was Lord of Brayington. His politics were wrong, it seems, and he was gently escorted out of England minus his title and most of his estates. His son, Salathiel Griffith, however, was appointed Lord High Sheriff of lower Maryland and upper Virginia under the King's commission. Later he served in the American Revolution. After the war he settled down to a planter's life in Virginia. My grandfather was a Captain in the American Army in the War of 1812, and his son, my father, fought as a young man in the American Army against Mexico, returning home to marry Mary P. Oglesby, whose father, Thomas B. Oglesby, had married Nancy E. Carter, of Virginia's famous Sherley Carter clan.

Several years after the '49 Gold Rush had begun, my father, as Captain of the Lone Jack Unit, convoyed the longest wagon train ever to cross the plains to California in that hectic period. The trip was successful despite such hardships and hazards as following dimly blazed trails, crossing flooded rivers, fighting Indians, etc. After two years of adventures in the Eldorado of the West, he returned to Kentucky.

Father was middle-aged when the War Between the States broke out. He joined the Confederacy and as Colonel Jacob Wark Griffith commanded the First Kentucky Cavalry and earned the brevits of the brigadier general. The latter title was never used by his intimates.

After Bull Run, father was known as "Roaring Jake Griffith" to his men and to General Joe Wheeler, a trusted officer. One night around a campfire, General Wheeler and father agreed that the first child born to either after the war would be named for the other. So one of my sisters went through life receiving no little mail addressed to "Mr. Wheeler Griffith."

Father was five times wounded during the Civil War, once was left for dead on the battlefield, virtually disemboweled by a shell explosion. Later, he was found by an army surgeon. An emergency operation in those days was a grisly affair, particularly for the soldiers of the Confederacy. The powerful Union blockade had prevented the South from having even proper surgical thread. So there on the battlefield, held down by assistants, the surgeon sewed father up hit or miss. They say he bit through his old gray felt campaign hat.

Major General Lord French, who commanded the British expeditionary forces in France during the early fighting of the late war, once told me a story that I had never heard before about father. British officers, it seems, make a most minute study of our Civil War history. Lord French said, "Your father was the only man who, to my knowledge, ever led a cavalry charge in a buggy. And a most successful one too!"

Suffering from a festering shoulder wound, he was about to lead a charge at the Battle of Corinth in Tennessee when he received a Minié ball through his hip. Unable to mount a horse, he turned the charge over to a subordinate. But when he saw his troops preparing to go into the fray without him, the fires of battle flamed high in the Old War Horse. Commandeering a horse and buggy, he rushed to the front of the long curved line of sabers sweeping down the field, leading the charge in person. This was a moving picture indeed . . . a hatless, middle-aged man, his long beard flying in the wind; around him the roar of battle; behind him his charging troops . . . while he, in a careening buggy, rockets into the jaws of death, his great voice calling down the wrath of God and Lee upon the enemy.

Then came black days for the Confederacy. After the hitherto invincible Lee's surrender, the first Kentucky cavalry was chosen to escort Jefferson Davis, President of the Confederacy, out of the country. The small body of Confederate soldiers struggled and maneuvered with their prize against the 62,000 Union cavalry of General Sheridan. Their efforts were in vain and father surrendered at Irwinville,

Georgia, May 10, 1865—a month and a day after the surrender of General Lee.

Like many others, father had staked everything on the Southern cause. He brought home a handful of worthless Confederate money. He also brought articles he had seized from the Yankees—a tattered uniform, a pistol, a saber. All these articles bore the inscription "U.S." So, strangely, the only relics we have of this ardent rebel bear the symbol of his enemies.

Father found the slaves gone, except for three extraordinarily large families who had calmly camped in various cabins with a childlike faith that "Colonel Jake" would take care of them. He found debts piling up and mother in broken health. He sold the land piecemeal to keep us going in fair style and even managed to maintain some spirit of culture.

As a small child, after having been sent to bed, I remember crawling cautiously back and hiding under the parlor table. I don't imagine it was so much to listen to father's literary readings as just to stay around with the grown-ups. A few neighbors would come in to gather round with the family and listen to father's dramatic readings from Shakespeare and other classics.

I got quite a little praise for my picture, *The Birth of a Nation*. Even Hollywood seemed to rather like it, but I think that that picture owes more to my father than it does to me.

The stories told of my father, particularly by veterans who had fought under his command, were burned right into my memory. I remember particularly one old soldier, Josh Long, of Crestwood, Kentucky. He said, "I believe if your father thought he had one drop of cowardly blood in his veins, he'd knife it out." Although he died many years after the war, it was the wounds and crude dressings that finally brought his death.

One could not find the sufferings of our family and our friends—the dreadful poverty and hardships during the war and for many years after—in the Yankee-written histories we read in school. From all this was born a burning determination to tell some day our side of the story to the world.

The tears of *The Birth of a Nation* were sprung in watching my mother on many a lonely night standing by a window waiting for someone's arrival—the arrival that would never be—and knowing of the thousands of other Southern women who had waited in vain for the return of their loved ones. Its drama was but an echo of the stories told of the gallant soldiers who fought one of the most brilliant wars known to history.

Underneath the robes and costumes of the actors playing the soldiers and night riders, rode my father—on his head the crested cap of courage. This is what I mean by saying that that picture owed more to my father and his gallant comrades than to myself.

When I think now of the fortunes amassed by the actors, producers, and writers in the moving picture business; when I read of their palaces in Hollywood, of their strings of race horses, polo ponies, yachts, etc.—my thoughts go back to a day long past, when as a child I witnessed my first magic lantern show. For after all, this "marvelous, stupendous" motion picture is only an improvement on the old magic lantern.

Imagine a winter night. There is snow on the ground. Vision an old schoolhouse, a very small one. On the eaves of its windows icicles glitter in the light of lanterns held by groups of farmers. Two steps lead up to the entrance through which the little groups throng. Then the magic entertainment begins!

While the views shown were mostly educational or religious, they were quite exciting to my childish mind. Of course, I didn't dream that the heir of this magic lantern was to make me fairly widely known around the world.

I sat by my father's side—by my hero. I didn't hold his hand because he always preserved an old soldier's reserve and dignity. Just the modulated tenderness, however, that came into his commanding voice when he called me "Son" seemed to bring all the glory and happiness there could be for me. To sit close to him and feel the warmth of his great body was as much rapture as a childish heart needed.

In this little entertainment that was given at the schoolhouse that night there was, besides the magic lantern show, an exhibition by a strong man. To me, this seemed as exciting and interesting as the magic lantern entertainment.

In the dim light from the lanterns placed around the little school platform, this mighty man bared his hairy chest. He placed his body across two chairs and his assistants laid a huge rock upon him. It covered his entire chest. True, he did have a piece of leather between the rock and his flesh, but this appeared very thin indeed. Then one of the assistants took up a heavy sledge hammer. The hammer fell. Crash! Again and again. You could hear the ring of steel on stone resound through the little room. The audience was spellbound. I remember to this day how the strong man's whole body seemed to quiver and shake. It seemed almost about to break in two as each blow of the sledge hammer fell. What drama! What suspense! Could that human frame endure the agony until the rock was broken? He, the strong man, had promised that it would be done, but could he fulfill the promise?

We watched and hoped. Then again the hammer fell. We wanted someone to stop it, and yet again, we wanted the struggle to go on until the strong man won. Finally, there came a terrific climactic smash of the sledge hammer and the rock actually split, the fragments falling to the floor. So the scene ended happily to the great applause of the onlookers.

It still seems to me to this day that the drama of the strong man fighting the rock and sledge was as thrilling as any I have ever seen since. Certainly, none has ever impressed me more than this contest in the old country schoolhouse.

Many years later, when I was making the picture *Way Down East* with Lillian Gish and Richard Barthelmess, it was necessary to introduce into the picture as much pastoral beauty as possible. Not only in this picture but in all others where similar scenes were required, I tried to find a scene that would match a vivid memory of our old farm down in Kentucky.

There was a small field close behind that farmhouse. I went out to it early one spring morning, when a boy, with a little pail to gather dewberries. The berry patch was on a gently sloping hillside. Behind it was a double log cabin where lived two Negro families that had been slaves of my parents. Beside the rambling cabin flowed a small stream and on one side of the patch there was a stake-and-rider rail fence. Several larks were soaring up and down from this rail fence, singing ecstatically in the clear spring morning. In memory, I always seem to see around this entire scene a luminous glow of joy. As I walked, it seemed that my bare feet hardly touched the ground. Of course, I did not realize then that never again would I know such pure joy, such singing, soaring ecstasy as that which my childish heart knew that spring morning long ago.

Often afterwards, I have thought what a grand invention it would be if someone could make a magic box in which we could store the precious moments of our lives and keep them with us . . . and later on, in dark hours, could open this box and receive for a least a few moments a breath of its stored memory.

There were innumerable darkies around our old Kentucky home and, as a rule, where these people are, so are music and laughter. I particularly remember one old broad black mammy whom we called "Aunt Easter." She lived in a cabin on the place, nearly two miles from our house. Occasionally, I would trot over and visit her. There were only two rooms but both were spotless and Aunt Easter made hoe cakes that would have your mouth watering as she baked them right on the embers of the fireplace. The butter on those hoe cakes was always borrowed from mother, but somehow, they always seemed to taste better than at home.

Then there was Uncle Henry. During the four years of the Civil War he had been father's body servant and had returned home with him to live on the place. Looking backward, it seems that father enjoyed his company more than that of any other member of his own family. Perhaps they had been tossed so close together by the many hardships of war that they had more in common.

Uncle Henry trimmed my eldest brother's hair one day. This was when men wore their hair long. But Uncle Henry cut Brother Will's hair after today's style—very close and round cut in the back. Father appeared upon the scene towards the finish of the job and Uncle

Henry queried: "Like it, suh?" Father bellowed: "Like it! Why, you've ruined my best looking son, you black — —!" Father then dashed into the house, fetched out his old saber, and proceeded to chase Uncle Henry around the yard with many a "desperate" thrust and slash of the weapon while Uncle Henry laughed his fool head off as he ducked from tree to tree. Finally making his escape, Uncle Henry returned with a pot of glue and, with mock gravity, began picking up the locks of hair strewn around and pretending to paste them back on my brother's shorn head. I relate this incident merely to stress the peculiarly close relationship between the whites and Negroes of the old regime. It was beyond my powers of description.

Sometimes, there also came a most welcome visitor—at least, to the children. This was an old Jewish peddler who carried an enormous load on his back as he walked through the countryside. From memory he does not appear as a good businessman as it was his custom to lay out his pack of varied stores and let the family take what they wanted. He never seemed to push the sale of anything.

One late winter evening he stopped overnight with us. There was a blazing fire on the large hearth and overhead a row of apples hung on strings, slowly turning as they roasted and filled the air with their aroma. The old peddler sat in a corner by the fireplace, took a small old accordion from his pack, and began to play strange airs. He seemed to enjoy this very much and we young ones loved it. He would pause to tell stories of his travels and then return to his accordion.

There was a double thrill in all this for the children. Not only did we enjoy the entertainment, but the family allowed us to stay up much later than usual. The old peddler loved his music and there was a strangely abstract smile on his face while he played on. Then he seemed like a painting of some old patriarch in the family Bible.

Later in life I became well acquainted with Rabbi Myers of a Los Angeles synagogue. Although it is a far cry from the little peddler of my childhood, trudging his lonely way through country lanes, to Rabbi Myers, a learned scholar, there was something about both . . . an aloofness from petty mundane matters . . . that they shared in common.

Rabbi Myers was the father of beautiful Carmel Myers, who became a famous movie star. Her father brought her to me one day and I promptly gave her a place in our company.

The rabbi became a member of our research department while we were making *Intolerance*, a religious picture. He was a poor man and yet, on payday, when everybody else in the studio would be lined up for the welcome envelope, Rabbi Myers, books under one arm and the contents evidently swimming around in his head, would invariably forget all about the pay envelope and mosey on his way home. We would generally have to get someone to take it to him. He was a dear old chap.

Visits were often exchanged between our family and relatives from Shelby County, some fifteen miles away. This was quite a distance in those days when you had to depend on the horse for transportation.

Among these relatives was the Honorable John White's family. After the war, Cousin John managed in one way or another to keep his fine farm. His hobby was politics; in those days it was called "statesmanship." Quite often, the most casual remark made by Cousin John became an oration. It seemed impossible for him to express the manner in which he wanted an egg boiled without becoming oratorical. However, he was understood to have been quite a brilliant fellow.

As a child, I remember having breakfast at his house when he pompously quoted several Latin phrases from one of the classics. His eldest son disputed the veracity of his quotations. Cousin John banged the table with his fist, rattling the dishes and knocking several to the floor, as he stormed in a dogmatic voice about the general "cussedness" of modern youth. "Imagine a son," he thundered, "correcting his own father—and in the presence of guests! Things were different in the old days."

Cousin John was the author of about the most laughable metaphor I have ever heard. He and the famous J. C. P. Breckinridge once engaged in a political debate in the county courthouse. Senator Breckinridge had made a caustic remark about Cousin John's knowledge of the law, and Cousin John, in rebuttal, waved his arms in sweeping, high-flown gestures, declaiming: "Senator Breckinridge slurs me before this brilliant assemblage by casting aspersion on my legal erudition. . . ." Rising to the climax with slow, heavy emphasis on each syllable, Cousin John thundered:

"My knowledge of the law as compared to that of J. C. P. Breckinridge is as the refulgence of the midday sun to the infinitesimal light on the tail-end of a glow worm!"

These were not Cousin John's exact words. Ladies did not attend political meetings in those days and the language was much franker. At any rate, they say that this grandiloquent "brought the house down."

Then there was Aunt Becky Oglesby. She was an astute business-woman and, in that respect, very unlike my mother. Aunt Becky was but a mite of a woman; a small yardage of alpaca completely filled with brains and energy. She sent four sons and two daughters through college, literally over a path of butter and eggs. What a grand story her life would have made. She rode around in an old buggy, the harness tied together with strings . . . everything must be saved for the children. All her sons attained some measure of fame. One became Senator Woodson R. Oglesby of Lenox, Massachusetts, and Park Avenue, New York City. Of the others, one became a banker, another a doctor, and the remaining one entered the ministry.

Aunt Becky was deeply religious and fully trusted in the Lord, but unlike most, she refrained from placing all her burdens on His shoulders. She kept plenty on her own tiny shoulders and struggled under them courageously.

At the time of my father's death, I was ten years old, the youngest in a family of seven with tremendously varying ages. My elder brothers and sisters were old enough to have been my parents.

After father's death came the deluge. Mother learned he had been paying ten percent compound interest on several mortgages and that we were now among the poorest of the poor. The old wolf, whose mournful whine had been heard at the doors of so many unfortunates, now made a personal appearance in our back yard. Everything was on my poor mother's shoulders. Before the war she had never done work of any kind. Now, she was at it from dawn to dark—and then some. She even made the clothes I wore. And I often think of the contrast between the little suit she made for me and the one I had tailored years later for my meeting with Alexandria, Queen Mother of England.

In my life—in common, I believe, with most unhandsome men—I have taken a great interest in clothes. Early in youth, I made the unhappy discovery that I couldn't do anything about my face. I would feel perfectly beautiful inside but the mirror would not agree with me. After hours of study before these instruments of torture, I would inevitably find that, no matter how I postured, my long nose was still just as long and the general contour of the "old map" was always the same. It was mine and I was stuck with it. So I began taking a great interest in clothes, thinking to decoy the fair sex as much as possible with "glad" raiment.

There were two sartorial gems that I remember best: One was gotten up for me by one of the best tailors and outfitters in London; the other was a blue homespun rig made by my mother for me when I was a child.

The first outfit was tailored for an appointment with Queen Mother Alexandria and Queen Mary of England. At that time, my motion picture, *Intolerance*, was running at the old Drury Lane Theatre. I had just made arrangements with Lord Beaverbrook, minister of information for Great Britain, to produce movies for the propaganda department of the Allies.

Now I was going to meet the Queens! Filled with dreams, I was determined to make an impression on these great ladies . . . one that they would never forget. In fact, I was mentally already right in the bosom of the royal family.

There was no lack of advice on tailors. Incidentally, Lord and Lady Cholmondeley, two of the grandest people alive, helped me in this matter. Lord Cholmondeley is still one of the handsomest, as well as best dressed, men in England.

So, dressed in what I considered the *ne plus ultra* of sartorial splendor, I was introduced to Their Majesties by Lady Mary Paget, one of the Queen Mother's intimates.

The Queen Mother was one of the world's beautiful and gracious women. She made it a point not to be out-done in graciousness, even by the lowest commoner. Not being well posted on Alexandria's court etiquette, I bowed when she bowed. She would smilingly make me another bow and I would return the compliment, wondering how long I could keep up this sort of thing. I bobbed up and down so many times I got a crick in my back before it dawned upon me that a queen is supposed to have the last bow.

The other outfit, the homespun rig, had a cap to match and I thought it "a darb." Highly proud of my new suit, I took a trip from Crestwood to Louisville, some eighteen miles. Doubtless, I misinterpreted the smiles of other passengers in the coach as stamps of approval. And it was while wearing this homespun suit that I committed the only purely unselfish act of my life.

In common with all persons who become fairly well known in the world, I have given away a great deal of money to public charities, etc. On close analysis, however, it is difficult to find whether I did this through unselfish motives or not. Even when you give or lend money to an individual without publicity, you always achieve a certain glow of satisfaction, thinking, "What a grand guy am I." That is reward enough in itself, but I believe that in my childhood I performed one really unselfish act and am perfectly willing to brag about it.

It was a mile-and-a-half hike to my old schoolhouse. It was just after father's death and we were very poor. About the cheapest provender that could be scared up for my lunch was apple butter, as we had plenty of apple trees on the place. This apple butter was made in the fall and rationed out during the winter. By late winter this cheap mixture became quite sour and difficult to swallow. But it was the best we could afford.

Mother would make me a simple luncheon consisting of a few slices of bread and a cup of apple butter. The bread was all right but the apple butter was hard to take. Looking at the brown mess in the cup, I would be tempted to throw it all away, but upon reaching home, mother would always ask if I ate my lunch. I couldn't hurt her feelings, so I ate the stuff religiously. Times change. Since then I have been awarded the mantle of Ananias on numerous occasions.

Conditions went from bad to worse on the old estate and we were soon forced to give it up. We moved to Shelby County, Kentucky—to what, I am sure, was the most useless farm in the entire world. It seems that my eldest brother was guilty of buying this farm because of a pretty face next door. Shortly afterward, he married the girl. Until I was twelve, we waged a losing fight against rocks, roots, bugs, and worn-out soil, in a desperate attempt to pay off an $1800 mortgage. We never made a dent in it.

From our new home we went to a school about two and a half miles away. In later years I have often thought that this was the cause of why I did not grow up overly bright. It seems that as time rolled on and the family kept moving that the schoolhouses kept getting farther and farther away from me. This particular one was near the village of Southville. We had to ford a winding stream seven times in making our way from home to schoolhouse. But we went to school, rain or shine, sleet or snow.

Those were the busy days: Up before daylight and milking the cows; general chores around the house and then a two-and-a-half mile tramp to school. In good weather, we enjoyed it, but in the event of rain or snow we always arrived at our destination thoroughly drenched and chilled to the bone. Then we would have to sit on our hard benches and depend upon the small stove or the mercy of the good Lord to dry us and prevent pneumonia. Here my first real battles with life began. In retrospect, it seems to have been a constant war in miniature.

During the last years of the World War, I was fortunate enough to hear at first hand the conversation of such men as Lloyd George, Bonar Law, and Lord Beaverbrook, concerning the possibility of a lasting peace. They all seemed to believe that the war then going on would end all wars, at least for a long term of years. Looking back over my youth, however, I am inclined to believe that the chance for a permanent peace in this crazed world is slight, indeed. There seems to be inherent in all of us the liking for a good fight. For example, when I first started to this little country school in Shelby County, the other boys made it pretty hot for me. Whether it was because I was a stranger in the community or whether it was just the general cussedness of my own disposition, I am unable to say. Anyhow, the boys went after me pretty strong.

At this period I had acquired a good Christian spirit and actually strove to follow the teachings of nonresistance that had been impressed upon me by my mother and other members of the family who, particularly after father's death, clung in their despair more earnestly than ever to religion.

One rather hard-boiled youngster, incidentally, the tollgate keeper's son, once socked me on the cheek. Following my religious training, I actually turned the other one. He whooped and walloped that side, too.

One cold afternoon this same youngster gave me a swift kick in the pants. Losing a struggle with my conscience, I finally started in to repay him in worldly fashion. We tussled, and he was fast beginning to realize an ambition to crack my skull against a tree when I grabbed him by the hair. Suddenly, I saw bobbing out from under that woolly, dirty, thatch, a crop of large fat lice. It turned my stomach upside down. I stopped struggling and tore away from him, brushing the vermin off my hand. Gamin jeers followed me. "He can't fight nuthin'."

These boys all came from what is termed "good, clean American stock." They came from families of allegedly high moral principles and, of course, churchgoing people. There was one lovable "good, clean, young American" who seemed to bear a particular grudge against me. If there was any part of my anatomy that missed his slaps and kicks, I don't remember where that fortunate part could have been.

Finally, I put up some resistance—to the great joy of the other boys of this young Society of the Brotherhood of Man, who looked on gleefully while we tore up the turf. Much as I would like to recount one victory, the truth must out. We wrestled, kicked, and walloped each other, and I got the worst of it. But this show of resistance did seem to ease matters up for a while.

This talk of war to end all wars and bring about a lasting condition of peace is so much hokum. The boyhood experiences recounted above and added to many others—directing mobs in the movies, watching the conduct of human beings as they slaughtered each other in the Great War, plus quite a close association with myriad tramps and hoboes—force me to the conclusion that the majority of people prefer most anything to peace.

By the way, while I did have a few hot arguments and fewer fights among tramps and hoboes, I found them on the whole to be a pretty nice sort. Perhaps their bitter struggles with the world and hiking constantly hand-in-hand with failure and despair had tempered their spirits somewhat. They seemed to possess a sort of fatalistic philosophy and tried to get along with everyone with as little friction as possible.

About the country boys, however. Today the movies are accused of corrupting the morals of youth and contributing to the "degeneracy of modern adolescence." This is all so much baloney. The sex morals of some of these country youths of my day were lower than a snake's belly. They had never read obscene books, certainly had never seen a motion picture, yet their conversation and actions were unprintable. While I am not in an authoritative position, I believe from observation that the youth of today is a much better class.

My memory of the old schoolhouse is somewhat shadowed but there were one or two bright lights that stand out. All my life I have been accused of being a devoted admirer of the opposite sex and somewhat of a connoisseur of feminine pulchritude. People have often asked, "Who was your first star?" They remember the Gish girls, the Talmadges, Mary Pickford, and many others who were with me during my career; that I made the screen tests for Claudette Colbert of the present order; that Norma Shearer, in her early days, was with my company. But they say, "Who was the first?" Well, there is a memory of one who was not exactly a star, but she was the first.

We had a favorite game played at recess called "Prisoners' Base." The woods outside the schoolhouse were quite beautiful—silver-barked beech trees and, in the fall, banks of golden leaves. On nice clear autumn afternoons we had a barrel of fun playing this particular game.

37

There was one. A slim nut-brown maid with curling chestnut tresses. Her name I have, of course, forgotten. But I do remember that she often wore a red cap and my vision of her running tauntingly from her "camp" over to mine, and then flashing away from us all through the autumn woods, is still clear and dear. Of course, I loved her. But I was not all original in this. Most of my school fellows were in the same boat. How she would speed from tree to tree, now running near to us, now away—those brown locks glinting as her slim legs twinkled by! Man! I am here to tell you that I wanted her on our side.

For hours at a time, I have had to stand on motion picture studio sets and also walk miles looking for good locations, and often I have been complimented on the stamina and endurance of my legs. No credit belongs to me. It all goes to the little nut-brown maid. I must have run that female countless miles playing "Prisoners' Base." And she was certainly a speedster, for I never overtook her. Of all the enticing ladies I have known, on or off the stage, none is more vivid in memory—and none has caused me more musing and anguish—than this little maiden under the beech trees of long ago.

One summer I helped my elder brother, Jacob, a most lovable visionary. He was heroically attempting to eke a living out of a weekly newspaper in the nearby hamlet of Smithfield. Subscriptions were paid mostly in produce and looking backward it seems that squashes and pumpkins formed the principal items in these payments. At that, we were conceivably overpaid. Later, Jacob became the publisher of several small-town newspapers, his last being the Whittier (California) *Register*. He turned this latter weekly into a daily and, I believe, had lots of fun with it.

About this time—we were still poor as country church mice—I remember mother conversing with the neighbors when someone brought in the name of Astor. Mother paused over a mess of embryonic corn bread, our principal food then, and commented, "Oh, yes—those fur traders from up North."

The Astors perhaps had their side of this point. These people of mine, however, had raised blooded horses and other stock, and pedigrees were all important.

There was no honorable career open to the youngsters of my day but gentlemanly farming, ministry, and the law. The law, of course, was considered a stepping stone to "statesmanship." Writers, if they didn't slip their traces, might amount to something. But the stage!

To go into business merely to make money was frowned upon. It took me many years to discover just how silly this idea was. Many good, sound American dollars slipped through my fingers that I could use right now, and all on account of that poisonous belief. In that day, however, the newly rich Astors and Vanderbilts meant little to the beggared aristocracy of the South. In later years I became acquainted with some members of the Astor and Vanderbilt clans and realized that they were the social leaders of America, but the jibes I had heard from the old families down in Kentucky kept recurring and made it difficult for me to give them whatever obeisance they deserved.

The Griffith family finally gave up the long daylight-to-dark fight on the farm to move to Louisville and give the younger children a better chance for an education. Excitement reigned in the little farmhouse. We were going to live in the city! No more back-breaking toil in the tobacco patch; no more yanking a two-horse plow around row ends; no more struggles with obstinate cows—of all females, the most "ornery"; no more tediously long farm chores. We were going to the city—hooray! hooray!

What an entrance! Right into the city of Louisville we trundled with our furniture piled on top an old two-horse wagon. I was piled on top of the furniture. From all sides, as we slowly creaked and rattled towards our new home, came jeering cries from street urchins.

"Country jakes! Country jakes!"

Part Two

DIRE POVERTY trailed the Griffith family right into the new home in Louisville. The old wolf who had haunted us so long now moved right in, fangs and all.

There were many prominent men who had known my father well and whose friendship I could have used to good ends. But I was ashamed to cloud father's reputation by letting his friends know that I was his son.

Among father's friends were the famous J. C. P. Breckinridge and Colonel Julius Haldeman, owner and publisher of the *Louisville Courier-Journal*, and Sallie Ward Downs, the famed belle of Kentucky. The latter approached me while I was working as "cash-boy" in a cheap dry goods store and inquired if I were not Colonel Griffith's son. Happily, a domineering clerk yanked me out of this dilemma by yelling, "Cash-boy! Come on with that change!" in such an explosive tone that I scampered over to him and was promptly weighted down with some material and shoved down the basement steps towards the wrapping desk. So my duties saved me from an embarrassing situation.

When about fifteen I was met with a crisis. Of course, you understand I was quite an "old man" by this time and had met many crises in a long life. But this was, nevertheless, a real one. I was forced to immediately decide whether to continue at school and add to my already massive education or go to work and bring home the much needed bacon to the family fireside. Personally, I didn't approve of either of these ideas, having for some little time entertained the thought that perhaps some unheard of uncle rich as Croesus would hear of our plight and promptly mail me a million-dollar check special delivery.

That would make everything "jake," enable me to see the world, and, of course, meet The Girl. She would be beautiful . . . everything. And she would be true to me, so true—all five thousand of her. But now I had forcibly arrived at the conclusion that this miracle was not going to pass. So I decided to get the job.

After making a thoroughly scientific investigation, I decided to try acting. From all reports, the business of treading the boards offered the best means of making a living without running into any danger of prostration from overwork. In the interest of field research, I saw my first theatrical performance. It was *America's National Game* starring Pete Baker at Macauley's Theatre. A few weeks later I had saved enough pennies to see Julia Marlowe in *Romeo and Juliet*. And the die was cast. But there was no chance of getting a job in the acting business at that time, so I worked at all sorts of petty jobs—cash-boy, elevator boy, vinegar peddler, book salesman.

Then later I got a job in Flexner's bookstore. Bernard, or "Ben," Flexner was the head of the store. Afterward, this family won no little fame and the name was widely known the length and breadth of the nation. Besides Ben, there were Washington and Jacob who prospered. Mary Flexner wrote several plays that were produced on Broadway. Of course, most renowned of all was Simon Flexner, who became head of the research department of the Rockefeller Foundation.

The Flexners were gentle, cultured people and the intelligentsia of Louisville and the countryside usually gathered in the back room of the store after closing hours to talk of mighty subjects. To this literary round table came such names as James Whitcomb Riley; Mary Johnson, author of *To Have and to Hold*; Adolph Clauber, a cousin of the Flexners who kept a photographic shop next door and later became dramatic critic of *The New York Times* and the husband of Jane Cowl.

It was my job to dust off the rows of books shelved in the store, but the only ones that got well cleaned were those near the table where mighty discussions were under way. I owe much to the Flexners and treasure many gentle memories of them. During all the time I was with them, although I am sure I needed many a good "calling-down," I received but one admonition from "Mr. Ben," who once said, "David, I don't blame you for wanting to read the books, but don't you think you should give a little time to dusting them, too—at least, during working hours?"

Louisville at that time was quite a place. There was Macauley's Theatre where all the best dramatic and light opera companies played. There was the Fourth Avenue Theatre of the "ten-twent-thirt" melo-dramas. In the latter all the villains in the course of one season would spill veritable rivers of blood, spiced with multitudinous shootings and sword play. The producers of these plays dared anybody to sleep during their performances.

In many a moving picture house I have thought that the propri-etors should charge the patrons room rent. They were using them for sleeping purposes only. The dark corners were also havens for neckers. But in the old Fourth Avenue Theatre, Blaney and Woods tossed out the drama in chunks, they dared you to take even a little nod . . . for just as you would be about to commit such a heinous crime, out would come Jack the Ripper, a cigarette in his mouth, a pistol in each hand, and all three smoking as he diligently and everlastingly pursued Little Nell. Just as he was about to seize her, entered Handsome Jack the Hero . . . and then the fun began.

We the audience must have been as dumb as audiences generally are, because, after having seen a score or more of these dramas tossed off, we should have known that no bullet ever molded could slay Handsome Jack. Why, a ten-pound dumbbell would bounce off Hand-some Jack's brow and, though he fell prostrate in the first act, he would come skipping out in the second without so much as a single bandage or dab of iodine to suggest that he had encountered any trouble whatsoever. As for the various Nells who played the heroines, it was just a waste of words for the other characters to tell how virtu-ous and beautiful they were. You know that they were both the minute they came on stage and you glimpsed their blonde wigs.

Besides this temple of art, there was the burlesque theatre. To this theatre came all the champion prizefighters, boldly proclaiming to all and sundry that "Five Hundred Dollars" would be given to any local bully-boy who could stay with them four rounds without getting his block knocked off. Bob Fitzsimmons, weighing but 158, was more successful in this particular line of slaughter than any other prizefighter before or since. He kept it up several years. My good friend, Jack Dempsey, tried it a few weeks until a Carnera in Minneapolis was inconsiderate enough to earn quite a few plaudits by almost reversing the procedure. So Dempsey, being a smart fellow, left this career for others to follow.

Then there was the burlesque chorus . . . "the most beautiful girls in the world." These were the mamas of today's strip-tease artists.

The races, especially the Kentucky Derby, turned Louisville upside down annually and still does. Flowersellers lined the entire business section of Fourth Street. One fine spring morning stands out. The fragrance of violets was in the air, a new rain had washed away the coal smoke, and the air was clear and invigorating. Everyone, high and low, was talking horses, nothing but horses. Bootblacks, waiters, clerks, shopkeepers, race-horse men, touts—everybody had the Derby in their blood. It was Derby Day, and the usually quiet streets had been alive all night with teeming crowds of people. They would continue to throb and pulse tonight after the races were over. Everybody had tips, and strangely enough, would freely dispense these supposedly valuable tips to any one, whether he asked for them or not.

The streets were jammed with buggies, phaetons, smart carriages with beautiful horses and gleaming trappings, all carrying the gaily dressed crowd to Churchill Downs. There was Douglas Sherley, an aristocrat and aesthete, in a high red and black trap, driving the smartest of all high-stepping cobs. Behind him perched a footman in livery. Sherley had just entertained Oscar Wilde, sunflower and all.

There were tallyhoes with four-horse teams, the coach horns thrilling on the air. A sway of horses and rigs every now and then tooled around the old corner of Fourth and Main streets. What envy as I watched from the street the smartly dressed crowds perched high on the tallyhoes. Among them was my friend, Adolph Clauber, wearing a top hat over his raven hair and wide pale forehead. He had just finished playing a leading part in Mark Twain's *Puddin'head Wilson* with a first class company.

I was running errands then and too busy to see the famous Derby. In fact, though they were virtually at my door, I never did see the races. Belonging to a crowd that had to keep on the go to make a living, I had neither the money nor the time to spend on this sort of thing.

This was a man's day. And there were districts famous for their entertainment of King Man. There were about five blocks of houses given up for this purpose on Green Street; four on Tenth; many second- and third-class bagnios on Grayson and other side streets. All night long they went full blast. Some of the dance halls, saloons, and night tearooms (where tea was unknown) were expensively and garishly furnished. Here a thousand hostesses provided entertainment for lonely man. Nothing new, of course. Was it not written three thousand years ago that Jezebel let down a scarlet thread from her window that all men might see?

Young scions of the best families in the South had passionate affairs with these American geisha girls. They would be with them night after night; drinking with them, dancing with them, making torrid love to them; attracted like so many motes to a beam to the district where the red lights glowed like fireflies, where there was music, laughter, shouting, murmuring, and the sound of dancing feet. But if these young men met the same "sweeties" on Fourth Avenue, Louisville's principal thoroughfare, the very next afternoon, the girls would never dream of showing the faintest sign of recognition.

Many of these backstreet houris were renowned for their beauty among other things. It is unbelievable today, but I have seen society notices in the old *Louisville Journal* to the effect that "the beautiful Mlle. Marie 'Toinette, of New Orleans, is visiting Louisville and receiving friends at No. 718 Green Street." Prosperous ladies of the evening even had their own carriages and rode through the principal streets, flaunting their charms from under fluffy parasols.

The entrance to one of the cheaper class sin dens was usually through a long corridor. There would be a long bar on one side, tables on the other, and a dance floor in the rear. Near the entrance of the room was the customary piano where a dejected Mozart would bang away for countless hours. The top of the piano was generally decorated with a whisky glass or beer stein.

One cheap dance hall pianist I remember well. He played every sort of tune, and many of his own composition. Louisville musicians claim that it was he who originated ragtime, and to him they gave credit for syncopation. The composers of ragtime, swingtime, and all hot music owe a large debt of gratitude to this man. The tin pan alley champions who have become millionaires should erect a tall monument to the man who invented a new rhythm. Here was written "Frankie and Johnny"—but not for million-dollar royalties, only for the nickels and dimes that dropped into the cup on the piano, plus free drinks.

In the back rooms of these cheap dance halls one often saw an eager young girl, sparkling with life, going swiftly from place to place in search of a recalcitrant lover, or even some poor fellow who could afford nothing better than one bottle of beer at two bits a throw. The latter type would treasure this nectar as long as possible in order to gaze long and covetously at the feminine flesh displayed so bawdily just beyond reach.

In this man's world, the men themselves claimed that all this was according to the laws of nature. They cited the pastures where there was always one male to many females; the barnyard, where one rooster had a yard full of hens. Men were supposed to be true to their wives, but only after a fashion. They claimed also that their wives considered it beneath them to be jealous of this sort of thing. If the men dared an affair with women of their own class, then there was the devil to pay. But men were men, and the double standard was just a part of life in those days. How the women felt about it, I am unable to say. Of course, behind the footlights of all this alleged glamour there was suffering and disease. But that is another story.

Among the Decent Women of that day smoking was unknown. Nowadays, few eyebrows are lifted when top-ranking ladies are seen virtually inhabiting cocktail bars and smoking cigarettes chain fashion.

But in my day, if a nice girl was spotted taking a drink in any place even resembling a barroom—well, she wasn't a nice girl any more. And that was that.

The old dads of that bygone day had things fixed pretty well after their own ideas. Their wives, daughters, and daylight sweethearts must be beyond reproach. They were set up on pedestals to be admired and worshiped, but Lord help them if they did not stay on those pedestals. On the other hand, the old boys kept a world of women on tap whose sole business in life was to cajole, flatter, and entertain that lordly creature called "Man."

Women then had practically only two avenues open to them to make a decent living. One was to be a wife; the other, a hired girl. Today there are as many decent avenues open to women as there are to men. No longer must the girls get married in order to hold their heads up. And if they do marry and hubby begins cutting up, they can and do tell him promptly where to go, while they themselves wend serenely on their way to Reno and back to pick up where they left off.

Another side of life in those days that stands out in memory concerned the palace boats that plied between Louisville and New Orleans. Their long bars and ornate gambling saloons were always crowded with women of all classes and creeds. Here also the lines between the Nice Girls and the Other Kind were drawn as strictly as possible. There are many legends of the fortunes won and lost over palace boat gaming tables; of love adventures ranking with those of François Villon himself; of hot blood boiling over cards or women. Many duels were fought in famed Gamblers' Row at Lawrenceburg, Kentucky. This place won attention as a favorite dueling ground because, when quarrels on the palace boats mounted to the shooting point, it was proper etiquette for the principals to wait until the boat had landed to finish the affair of honor ashore. The owners of these mighty river queens were justly proud of them and, I suppose, objected to having their white gleaming decks strewn with practically useless bodies.

Adventure of this stripe found me on the sidelines. A poor boy had little chance at this sort of thing.

47

Finally the great opportunity came. I received a chance to go on the stage! For two years now I had been taking vocal lessons from Mr. Baustead, a popular music teacher of that day in Louisville. He assured me that I possessed one of the most powerful voices he had ever heard. His wife agreed in this by commenting, "Yes, it's powerful enough!" I didn't care for the way she underscored "powerful."

This stage opportunity came to me via one Ned Ridgely. Ned was a sort of steamboat comedian and small-town barnstormer; a little, cocky, glib-tongued Irishman. He had in tow a stage-struck blacksmith, Jim White, whose hands were usually as black as his hair. Jim was a burly old bull in appearance, but proved a good fellow. How his placid nature had ever become inflamed by the histrionic torch is still beyond my comprehension, although I suspect Ridgely.

It seems that the blacksmith had a bank account of $75—enough to get a stage company together. It was Ridgely's idea to inflict this company on small towns around Louisville for a little loose change. It seemed unbelievable, but the fact remains that Ned gave me a leading part. The little stage manager had been frank in telling me that "we are going out on a shoestring but, once started, there's no telling how far we might go . . . Look at McIntyre and Heath in *The Hamtree*. They started in a livery stable, too, in Henderson, Kentucky. Now look at them!" I had looked at them and it had cost me a quarter to sit in a "seventh heaven" top gallery in a regular theatre. "Sure," rambled Ned glibly, "that's why I say that we can't tell where we'll end. . . . The cards say this is a lucky venture."

At that time, I did not know what "going out on a shoestring" meant . . . so I went around Louisville bragging about it. The star was to be the blacksmith, but after him, I had the next leading part. Rehearsals were held in a small room behind the blacksmith shop and our wild histrionic shoutings were punctuated rythmically by the assistant blacksmith hammering out iron in the adjoining shop.

When I announced to the family circle that, at long last, I was an actor, poor mother took me gently aside and informed me that great-grandfather had claimed direct descent from those Griffiths who were the reigning family of Wales from the seventh to the thirteenth century; that during this period they had intermarried with most of the royal families of Europe; that after England conquered these same Griffiths in the thirteenth century, we have heard little from them in history, doubtless because they had in the interim committed variously assorted villainies . . . "but none is on record as having fallen so low as to have become an actor."

This was quite a mouthful to mull over, but, being seventeen, I knew it all—and away I went.

The name of my first company was "The Twilight Revelers." Our first engagement was played in the loft of a converted livery stable in Jeffersonville, Indiana, a small town across the Ohio River from Louisville, and we escaped alive. We also managed to assault three other hamlets but at the fourth, a village of some 900 inhabitants, met our Waterloo. Immediately after one performance, we actors were informed by the management that the board money had run out, "but if you all can escape this particular house, the next town is a *great* show town and everything will be hunky-dory."

That night the entire company attempted to forsake the boarding house via a rear second-floor window and a bedclothes rope. First out and down, I was promptly grabbed by the landlord—who loomed up in the night bigger than Jim Jeffries. One huge paw on my celluloid collar, he waited patiently for the others to slide down the makeshift rope. Before each went into his or her fireman's routine, he or she would stage-whisper into the night: "Catch my valise!" and down would plump a worn, scarred bag into the arms of the landlord. This majestic person cornered one and all and waited quietly until the last member had hit the ground.

The last fugitive turned out to be Ridgely, but, before the landlord could open his mouth, Ridgely had sized up the situation with some split-second thinking and promptly launched into a fiery line of patter about "the art and glory of the stage." Ned's "oil," however, worked too well. The landlord joined the company. He pointed out that he would go on with us to the next town and collect his board bill from the receipts of our performance there. It seems that he also had a secret yen to walk through a stage door unmolested.

Within a few weeks we had five landlords carrying spears for the art and glory of the stage plus Ned Ridgely and his blacksmith protégé . . . also the board bills. Towards the last, one of the landlords even put his gold watch, a biscuitlike family heirloom, in soak to keep the show's head above water. Such a Utopian scheme to save the theatre, however, was doomed to failure.

On one never-to-be-forgotten night, several of the landlords' ever-loving wives appeared out front in a body instead of the cash customers, and this dual tragedy proved too crushing a blow for Ridgely to weather. So, for the first time, but by no means the last, I was forced to beat my way back to Louisville and home. But now . . . now . . . *I was an actor.*

Once home I soon learned that Thomas Coffin Cooke, the stage director, was going to put on a play in Louisville. The play was *The District School*, and he gave me the role of the dunce. All I had to do was sit on a high stool two hours and remark once during every performance, "The breeze from the lake blows chilly tonight."

Was I good in that part? (I rather suspect that I have been playing it ever since.) But this show soon folded, and then I got a substantial part with a real company, the Meffert Stock Company. These people took in hard cash and actually paid their actors' salaries. And their leading people were the idols of Louisville.

After the matinees, whole coveys of fluttering belles waited outside the stage door for a brief close-up of their favorites. I bore this in mind while I rehearsed and rehearsed. My part was a heavy one, but not too heavy for me. Bursting with enthusiasm, I constantly annoyed the neighbors by shouting my lines in stentorian tones. The entire surrounding neighborhood soon learned the plot of the play. Some Weisenheimer suggested that I go to the park for my rehearsing. So I got out on a hill in Cherokee Park and began ranting.

Just as I was hitting on all sixteen, a policeman with wonder on his face and a gun in his hand appeared from behind the bushes. Several excited old ladies hung behind the cop. One yelled, "That's him! He's crazy!" Another cackled: "That man's been disturbing the neighborhood for hours. Lock him up!"

Even now I can feel the humiliation of that moment. It took a solid half-hour to convince the officer, and the complaining peasants, that I was an actor—an actor of the Meffert Stock Company, no less.

As the stock company gave two performances a day, we had little time for rehearsals. It seems, however, that I waded through them satisfactorily and invited everyone I knew and many I did not know to witness my initial performance. Of course, my mother and sisters would not come, but Jacob, with his lady friend and a small party, bought tickets for my Monday night premiere and prepared to give me a big send-off.

The great day came. At last I was on a real stage, acting. I knew my part and never dropped a word. In fact, in my enthusiasm, I added a few lines just to congeal the cheese. When my big dramatic scene came, I knew I had that matinee audience spellbound . . . or maybe earbound, anyway. Believe me, there was no one in that audience who did not *hear* me.

After the matinee I hesitated, bathed in perspiration, as I saw the manager advancing. He came up and presented me with one dollar and a half. (My weekly salary was "eight per.") I fancied that he had liked my acting so well that he intended paying me some in advance. I asked quickly "You liked it?" He responded quietly, "You are too grand for us." Then he said goodbye, and I knew then that I had been fired. It stunned me.

Fired after my first performance! I began to boil over and was just about to point out to this manager in the strongest terms that, among other things, he was a benighted ignoramus when I noted that he was over six feet and built like Colossus. So I ignored him . . . and tramped out the stage door in a high dudgeon of fine scorn.

Ashamed to go home and ashamed to be seen on the streets, I bought a sandwich and a new drink called Coca-Cola and then found an obscure poolroom and sat in the back for hours.

Thinking and thinking, I sat there envisioning my brother and his sweetheart waiting patiently for my entrance, the entrance that would never be. Occasionally, I would think of all the other people I had invited to be thrilled by my art. What a calamity! If I had only known

51

how to procure poison, I sincerely believe that I would have ended my agony then and there. Well, I got a lot of exercise out of the disaster. I walked the streets all night rather than go home.

Afterward, I got some "suping" jobs with various traveling companies. Once, I deified myself by carrying a spear for the divine Sarah Bernhardt. Standing in the wings, I would forget all about the old wolf as the golden voice of Bernhardt chanted those poetical lines. Despite her reputation she seemed quite gracious to everyone, even supers. But Madame insisted upon perfection in everything. When she was on stage there must be absolute quiet. Even the stage hands wore rubber-soled shoes.

One night a gaping extra, far up in flies above stage, was watching Madame Bernhardt. Trancelike, he leaned to one side to obtain a better view and succeeded in dropping about twenty pounds of armor. The crash knocked the lines out of Madame Bernhardt's head. She and her leading man stood horror-stricken for what seemed an eternity. They must have thought the theatre was being bombed. And it is best that the wretch remain anonymous for the spirit of this volatile actress might be on his trail.

When the final curtain fell, Madame Bernhardt wiped off the gracious smiles she had been bestowing on the audience and tore wildly into the stage manager. It was this poor fellow's duty to see that everything went smoothly backstage. Since it took us extras about an hour and a half to pack our costumes, collect our quarters, and dress for the street, I hung around and took everything in before starting for the stage door.

In one corner, the Divine Sarah, her smiles in limbo, had that little French stage manager backed against the wall. After a solid hour, she was still bawling him out. In rapid, fiery French, she gave him "the works" for nearly two hours. Madame's hands flayed the air; her whole body quivered; each hair on her head trembled as she eloquently excoriated the lout. He would try sneaking along the wall but she always headed him off. He would flee back to the corner and essay the other side. No dice. Madame was too quick. Next, he would face about like a cornered rat and try to alibi—but before he could open his mouth, the grande dame was on him with another machine-gun burst of invective . . . and so "far into the night." What a woman!

The next day during rehearsal the Divine Sarah alighted from her carriage and advanced through the admiring crowd that always awaited her and came on stage, bowing right and left like a gracious queen to her subjects. To her favorites she extended her hands to be kissed.

The stage manager halted the rehearsal and bowed low. She began advancing and I wondered why he didn't take to his heels. Then she opened a small box she was carrying and presented him with a beautiful gift, including several gold pieces. Madame kissed him on both cheeks and he returned the compliment with Gallic vehemence. They embraced fervently. Now, she consumed as much time and energy to apologize as she had the night before in berating him. Tears . . . raptures . . . forgiveness . . . joy. So I learned about women from Sarah Bernhardt, too.

Later, the Meffert Stock Company changed management. Oscar Eagle and his wife, Esther Lyon, took over and through Mr. Eagle's kindness I stayed on with them. When the theatre closed in early summer, however, I decided to storm the theatrical center of America —New York. Fevered by the virus of stage life, I sold my bicycle, drew out my savings, and with a sum total of $19 bought a round trip excursion ticket to Atlantic City. Selling the return ticket, I journeyed on roundabout to New York.

In all New York I did not know one person. For three days I lived in the shadow of the Brooklyn Bridge in a fifty-cent flophouse under the illusion that I was in New York City proper. It didn't take me long, however, to locate the theatrical agencies. And I haunted them for any kind of part. Soon, I was eking out a living by shoveling concrete. Finally, I was tossed a bone in the form of a part in one of the ten-twent-thirt melodramas of that day, but this show passed into the Great Beyond in Tonawanda, New York. So I became an ore shoveler and puddler in the Tonawanda Iron and Steel Company in order to ride the cushions back to Broadway.

Again I made the rounds and again I got a part in a melodrama.

This time it was *London Life*—booked from coast to coast. It was a fairly good company and I went to bed each night dreaming of California, that state of golden dreams. We started out boldly enough, but then our success began to peter out. We did a complete fold in Minneapolis.

My salary had been $25 a week during the several months of fair success with this company and I had lived cheaply, sending home a chunky slice of it weekly. But now pride stopped me from wiring home for aid. Doubtless, the family exchequer was running low, anyhow.

In subzero weather I crept into the blinds of a Chicago-bound baggage car and covered quite a distance before being booted off. After getting well thawed out in a roundhouse in company with a half dozen other hoboes, I hopped freights—trying the rods for awhile—and finally landed in Chicago, a well-frozen ham.

The next lap was the home stretch to Louisville. I trudged from Cermak and State streets towards Englewood fifteen miles away. The 'boes had posted me that this latter spot would prove the best chance for making the blinds. First, I stopped at a small tavern at Twenty-second Street. The place was well known to actors. It was a half block from the American Theatre stock company and its free lunch counter was famous. There I spent my last nickel for a small beer and promptly committed assault and battery on the free lunch.

With a slightly mixed provender safely inside me I hiked briskly to Englewood and managed to hop a fast passenger train bound for Louisville.

Grabbing the blinds is a little known art. You must wait until the brakeman has pulled in the coach doors and the train is fast picking up speed. Then you make a desperate leap for the rail handles on either side of the front of the baggage car, which is directly behind the locomotive tender. A slight miscalculation may put you in an unmarked roadside grave. Once aboard, however, and you're safe until the next stop, there being no way for the brakeman to get at you.

Huddled in an exposed blind baggage car with the bitter wind driving icicles clear through you is no picnic. And I had eaten exactly ten cents worth of food in three days.

After about eighty-five miles I was discovered by the brakeman that night at a water stop and unceremoniously kicked off. After hitting the hard-packed earth and cinders there was no resistance left in me. I laid there for some time—so done up that I was just about ready to call the whole thing off and stay there when some hidden reserve hoisted me to my feet and shivered me into a nearby village. After stumbling around the main street (my shoes were tied to my feet with rags), I found a Dutch baker who was just opening his shop in the early morning light. He let me toast my toes in his bake oven. For a few minutes thereafter the baker paid me no attention, but when he looked at me again he gave an astonished shout, "Ach! Gott!"—for I had crawled completely into the warm oven like Service's immortal Sam McGee. The Dutch baker—peace to his ashes—gave me twenty stale doughnuts. Nineteen I ate on the spot, making Louisville on the twentieth.

Years later, I employed this incident in W. C. Fields' *Sally of the Sawdust*.

In my off-and-on "jungle" life I found the shabby genteel character role that was tailored to order for Fields' perennial Micawber. Earlier, this sort of role was handed Charlie Chaplin, although this super-artist had brought virtually the same idea from London where, as a boy, he had studied the Micawber-like antics of the town soak who daintily held gentlemen's horses for tips.

After performing the minor miracle of scraping enough cash together, I landed in New York again . . . and on the Rialto once more. And again the flophouses claimed me. Compared to the old bugtrap by the Brooklyn Bridge, I had quite an elaborate apartment in this particular flophouse. There was a thin partition between another derelict and me. This chap was a confirmed devotee at the shrine of Bacchus and every night would puncture the foul air with numerous battle cries as he fought through horrendous struggles in his sleep. All this—added to the rattle, roar, and bang of the elevated and the raucous voices of the street below—was a far cry from the peaceful fields of old Kentucky.

The Ghetto, Mulberry Bend, the Bowery, and Chinatown were

all well known to me, but Rivington Street was the lively one, eternally jammed with pushcart peddlers hawking their wares. They had every imaginable commodity from a needle to a wedding outfit; even fruits and vegetables of all kinds in season. Rivington Street never appeared as a melting pot to me, but more like a boiling pot. Here were Italians, Greeks, Poles, Jews, Arabs, Egyptians, all hustling for a living. Emotional, tempestuous, harrowing Rivington Street was perpetually a steaming, bubbling pot of varied human flesh. And the Bowery by night! I would not attempt to describe it; that has been done by experts. But I knew every hot spot there.

Along this street could be heard pianos banging, violins screeching, braying instruments of brass, and every popular song of the day. Gaudy women swung in and out of doors of the various bagnios and bistros. Sometimes the street was alive with sailors ashore from the seven seas and avidly searching for life, women, drink, excitement. Maybe I passed the store where Irving Berlin hammered away on his inspired old piano. I did meet several, however, who came out of the Bowery to do good things.

The skin of the Bowery women was of every known hue. After the age-old manner of the siren, they chanted in many languages and accents the one hymn to lust . . . the same against which Ulysses had roped himself to the mast. That was one man who had the right idea. These women sang only to the cash register.

In those days a man was indeed lonely unless he had the necessary coin. Not having sprouted up with the pansies in the garden, I, like any natural young male, desired feminine companionship. There were no respectable clubs or places where the two sexes could meet conventionally. So I polished my shoes until they shone; brushed my suit and it also shone; set my hat on a rakish angle and walked mile upon mile. Away from the places where conversation and companionship were sold, however, it was a tough job. Not once did I attract the attention of even one lone female. Well, I imagine I was no Robert Taylor or Tyrone Power.

Once I managed somehow to get a little change in my pocket and visited the old Haymarket at Sixth Avenue and Twenty-seventh

Street, the rendezvous of the tenderloin. So into the Haymarket I strolled and up to a booth on the mezzanine where, from the cheapest section, I could look down upon the crowded dance floor below.

The first floor and other sections were largely given over to the real spenders. I was in the beer department. A young lady of scarlet stripe lounged over and invited me to have a drink with her—at my expense. We went into heavy conference, the momentous result of which was "Okay for a couple bottles of beer." Her pretty face clouded somewhat, but evidently seeing no "live ones" around, she accepted my companionship. She knew I wasn't going to put her in the carriage trade, but let it go at a couple bottles of beer.

After looking me over, she inquired sweetly if we grew alfalfa or just plain grass at home. I let this "sock" go over my shoulder and after a few sips of Dutch water confided—enjoining the strictest confidence —that I was no less than the son of an English lord. Later that evening I told her "the truth." I wasn't a lord at all; I was a royal duke and had lived in London all my life. She took this without a shudder, having been lied to by professionals. When she did get a word in edgewise, she began pointing out well-known New Yorkers on the floor below.

For all I know, she may have been romancing, but she pointed out certain individuals and tagged them with the surnames of the best families in New York. When she began calling out the famous spenders of the day, I became deeply interested. "See that fellow in the dark suit . . . the fat one?" I saw him. He was dancing with a pretty kid. My companion gurgled on with rapt expression: "Boy! If I could only make that lobster fall for me. Skidoo! Skidoo!" He was a corking dancer. "Say, country, you know that is the biggest spender in New York . . . Boy! When he throws a party you break your teeth on the pearls in the oysters he serves; you bruise your legs on the falling $20 gold pieces every time you lift a plate—and champagne! He serves it in tubs . . . Why, I knew a little floozie who went to one of his parties and made the waiters fill a bathtub full of champagne and then took a bath in it, guzzling bubble water at the same time . . . Gee! Look at the sparklers, would you! Diamonds all over him . . . Diamonds on his fingers . . . Diamonds for shirt studs."

57

As the room spun around, the dance music blared into a climax and she ecstatically breathed: "That's Jim Brady . . . *Diamond Jim!*"

Outside the fringe of the gaudy night scenes were dismal streets and alleys with beggars everywhere. Before dingy portals and in obscure nooks were dirty, greasy, unshaven bums . . . poor wrecks of humanity stretched out misshapenly on wooden steps or iron gratings, sleeping in their own filth. Sometimes they were alone, sometimes in little groups—dejected, shambling outcasts. They looked as if ghouls had taken shrouds from some slimy graves, put them on dummy figures, and mounted them with so many death's heads. For numberless days and nights I walked past these scarecrows of despair, quite sure in my heart that my end would be like their's had been.

Then I would go shivering "home" to my vermin-infested bed. Upon its gray covers were little red stains, revolting reminders of scrunched bedbugs. The air was fetid with their odor. Horrible phantom figures—even more horrible than those I had seen on the street—would appear and cluster around my flophouse bed, claiming me as one of their own.

How often was I assured in my soul that I would never get out of these grimy streets! I could even picture the kind of rags I would wear when I held out a cup to indifferent passersby . . . or the coming day when I would not have even the price of admittance to that nadir of existence, the five- or ten-cent flophouse.

The Bowery flophouses had cots arranged closely together in rows, upon which men made out of the image of their God reposed as best they could through hopeless nights. The wailing voices—shut the sounds out of your ears, for God's sake . . . shut the memories out of your mind . . . stop your thoughts, all of them, from whirling around and around. You must get some sleep . . . Do you hear the clock striking the hours? You have only a few hours now—then daylight . . . and Big Jim will pull the cord and your lousy cot, along with the rest, will flop to the floor and drop you into the filthy dust.

In 1903 I found myself in San Francisco. A company in which I had been playing had been shipwrecked, and again I was stranded. Every time I got fired during my struggles in the West, I went over and watched Lewis Stone's acting to try and solve what was wrong with my own. Today, Lewis Stone's pictures are famous around the world. At that time he was the best actor among the coast defenders and the matinee idol of the West.

It was here that I helped translate Helen Hurt Jackson's *Ramona* into a stage play with the part of Alasandra. Afterwards, the old Biograph Company purchased motion picture rights on this story for $15. What a bargain that would have been if we had bought it outright! Since then it has been produced in the movies three times. I made it once myself for Biograph with Mary Pickford and Henry Walthall. I played a short season in the West with Melburn McDowell and the patrons began taking well to his company. He grew prosperous and particular. I got fired. That happened in Portland, Oregon.

Seventy-five dollars was in the old sock and this sum was just about sufficient to get me back to New York. At last I was returning to the old Rialto again.

Various rosy reports of men throwing their last dollar on the gaming table and departing with a fortune had not missed my ears. After all, $75 would just get me to New York. And what a grand reception I would get from the boys if I landed in little old New York with my pockets lined with gold.

Luck, I felt, was with me. I would take $5 from my slim roll, visit one of the many gambling halls (all the West was wide open at that time), and come out with a young fortune. So I went in and battled the dice game. This is a very easy game quite unlike poker or bridge. It takes no brain work. There were only two movements to make: I put it down; the gentleman behind the table took it up. In less than one hour's time I had exactly seventy-five cents left. New York was lost to me and the next best place was San Francisco, castle of the coast defenders.

Signing on a lumber schooner, I worked my passage to the Golden Gate. I was to acquire plenty of experience on these lumber schooners. About this time I was offered a week's work with the Baker stock company in Portland. But after one had paid a round-trip fare from 'Frisco to Portland, it made quite a dent in the old salary check. So I determined to work my way there on another lumber schooner and save the fare. The schooner people and I were getting to be old friends by this time, and away I went. Soon I was to discover that the Pacific Ocean is pacific in name only.

Nearing Portland we ran into a towering gale. Fifty-foot combers were running and the small craft would slide down these huge waves, hit the trough bottom with a loud smack, then wallow from side to side to stagger up another billow. At the height of the storm with the wind shrieking magnificently through the rigging, I was exhilarated enough to burst into song. Right lustily I tore into "Many brave hearts are asleep in the deep—so beware . . . beware."

Suddenly, the song died a-borning as I was most rudely interrupted by the mightiest kick in the pants I've ever received. An extremely irate sailor and his mates were assailing my ears with the most indignantly profane and forceful invective I have ever heard. After getting my hips back into location, it dawned upon me that probably there was some cause for their indignation. My song—chaste and beautiful—was obviously not one for the occasion.

These superstitious sailors had nothing but scowls for me throughout the five days that the storm lasted. The lumber, lashed on deck, pounded constantly by wind and wave, now shifted. The schooner was listing badly. Unless the lumber could be gotten back in place, we were sure to sink. So lashing ourselves to masts, rails, or fittings, we worked desperately with long heavy crowbars, attempting to hoist these clumsy piles of lumber back in place. The cold gale lashed our faces and hands to numbness. And the sailors blamed me for everything, muttering: "You damned fool—that singin' of your'n riled the ocean . . . sailors hadn't ought to sing, no-how."

At last the storm abated and we crawled slowly into the Columbia River and up one hundred miles to Portland. Alas! The delay had been fatal. I was too late to get the part, and there was nothing else to do but catch the boat back to 'Frisco again. I sailed up and down the coast so often that I came very near embracing the sailor's life as my regular occupation. Strangely enough, the experiences I acquired, while not extensive, were sufficient to help me many years later to save my own life as well as thirty-two others, when on a sixty-foot yacht we struck a great blow in the Caribbean and were lost for six days.

Another disaster befell me in San Francisco. While working with a cheap road company, I had skimped and cut corners until I saved enough to buy a $45 post office money order. It was fastened tightly with two safety pins inside my vest pocket and, when we were eventually stranded and the improvident ones in the company were moaning low, I gloated over that forty-five bucks. I said nothing to anyone except my roommate, to whom I mysteriously hinted that everything would be all right. He was delighted as he, like the rest, was penniless. So we rented a cheap room and, after closing the door cautiously, I elaborately unbuttoned my coat and vest and fished for the money order. My heart dropped into my already overcrowded shoes. It was gone! Stolen! There we stood, speechless, fearing any minute that the landlord would knock and ask for the rent in advance. We had exactly one dollar and twenty-five cents between us.

Schopenhauer contended that "Happiness is only a surcease from sorrow." Well, the West Coast caused me enough grief to allow me a wide margin of surcease. It was here that a poisonous thought took possession of me. This thought was born in the dome of a close friend of Jack London. It came about when I was with the Central Theatre stock company and went without sleep for three days and nights. I would work matinees and evenings at the theatre and spend the rest of the nights at a table, listening to that mighty word juggler, Jack London, as he kicked the old world out of the window and swiftly hauled a magnificent new one in the door.

So, borrowing from London's friend, from now on when Dame Fortune jilted me, I would spit in her eye. In other words, if one suffered heavy reverses, throw what little remains into the breach and luck would be sure to return it manyfold. So every time the company failed me or I failed the company, I would take what few nickels I had left and sling a party for the boys. We would be wafted right out of the vale of misfortune as we regaled ourselves with drink and meat and, at least for a few hours, forgot our troubles.

It was about this time that the tide of my somewhat treacherous

61

fortune turned slightly for the better. Now came more substantial roles with better companies including Walker Whiteside, Nance O'Neill, J. E. Dodson, Helen Ware, and the Memphis and Neill Alhambra stock companies.

January 29, 1905, found me in the part of Sir Francis Drake in Paoli Giacometti's tragedy, *Elizabeth*, at Mason's opera house in Los Angeles. Years later, I was to return to that city to begin making motion pictures in a vacant lot at what is now Twelfth and Georgia streets. With the money from my Los Angeles engagement I managed to get back to New York and have something left. We thespians certainly did get around in those days.

Finding a lodging house on Thirty-seventh Street that was cheap but far superior to my former Bowery abodes, I stepped into my happiest days as an actor. It wasn't so lonely this time; I had one or two pals here . . . and I was beginning to quiet my heretofore growing alarm at the constant prospect of starvation.

This lodging house was the home of none but stage people, and what a place it was! From its many rooms accordions groaned, guitars tinkled, voices trilled the scales as one and all rehearsed over and over the popular tune of the day. Day and night you could hear the tapping of hoofers' routines and the mighty voices of Shakespearean actors rehearsing their lines. Fat actors liked this place. There was so little chance to sleep that they reduced as a matter of course.

The villain of all sleep-disturbing villains, however, was a cornet player. He would shame the most powerful calliope ever known. He tooted and tooted and blared and blared. Early one morning my roommate and I were trying to get some sleep and we finally rebelled against this cornet torturer. Dressing quickly, we knocked on his door, determined to cork him up or knock his block off. The door opened and we caught the villain red-handed with the deadly weapon of torture. To our astonishment, there stood a beautiful young girl evidently still in her teens. We apologized quickly and told her we had just dropped around to compliment her on her music. One of us hung around and tried to make a date, but the young lady was true to her cornet.

In the basement there was a grate where we hams did our own cooking. We clubbed together and one would buy a nickel's worth of butter; another, bacon; yet another, coffee. We would fry the bacon—that being about the most filling provender you could get for the money—and fall to. How the aroma of this bacon sizzling on the open coals smelled to these hungry actors!

We were hustling every day, trying to land a job. Every morning we hot-footed it over to Broadway to make the rounds of the agents. They wanted a tall leading man over at Brown's agency. I had two-inch lifts all prepared. Beginning with five feet, eleven inches, I made the quickest growth on record—six feet, one inch in a split second. Then over to Brown's fast. Bang! Into the office, acting as magnificently as possible, playing the desired part as I entered. Hope erased the pain in my back from the high heels.

The agent's reply to my eager inquiry would be:

"Sorry, but you're too tall."

"Why, Mr. Brown, I thought you wanted a tall man."

"Yes, that's so—but you're too tall for your width."

What could one do? One was virtually always too tall or too short, too lean or too fat, but that was the life.

Actors were then engaged either late in the summer or early in the fall. Both were gorgeous seasons in New York. There were many crisp autumn days for me on that enticing, make-believe street, the Rialto. There was youth, lifting its feet scornfully from the pavement in the clear, tangy air. Actors hurried from agent to agent or spieled magnificently in little groups about past contracts, while fascinating women swished up and down the street. There were dancing girls, singing girls, dramatic hopefuls. Their perfume filled the offices. Bright eyes sought to lure susceptible managers. For youth, this was the life.

For older people, however, the agents' rounds meant the usual disappointment, poverty, despair. But even they always kept at least a part of their youth in hoping for the good part that would surely come tomorrow—next week. Success was always just around the corner and hope put a glow over the dingiest lodging house. Hope was over the portals of every agent's doorway; over the sign of every tavern and restaurant. Hope gilded completely that silly, glamorous, foolish, adventurous Rialto of New York.

Night in the old boarding house found us hoping for adventure. There were some female charmers in the house, and we could hear doors opening and the thunderous rustle of dainty skirts in the hall. We watched for these lovelies, trying to snare their attention. But they would flit out of their rooms, down the hall, ignoring us entirely or merely dismissing us with a passing nod. Attractive young girls could always get a date somewhere for a regular dinner. Even a soda jerker could feed them better than we . . . so down in the basement we boys ate our bacon, celebrating whenever we got an egg to cook with it. We sipped our coffee and lied about how many women waited outside the stage door for us in Poughkeepsie or Albany during our last engagement. We would describe our feminine admirers so minutely that any but our own group would have swallowed it. We enjoyed it, trying to out-brag each other. If any actor was as good as we made ourselves out to be, what a treat the world would have! We would read lustily from our favorite parts, sing arias from our pet opera. A hoofer would show us right there on the kitchen floor how much better he could dance than George M. Cohan. Despite our troubles, I imagine there was as much jesting and horseplay going on among us clowns as there was anywhere in the great city of New York.

There was one young girl who did come down to the basement. She was slim and pale, possessing lustrous large brown eyes. She was a little beauty and there was no doubt about it. She would busy herself, fixing her own poor meal and then get in a corner alone and eat with her face turned to the wall. To us, she was Nanon, Helen of Troy, and Little Nell all rolled into one. I wrote her sonnets and songs, words and music, and even slipped some of my alleged poetry under her door. In my imagination I walked mile after mile with her, dreaming countless dreams of purple adventures of love in which she was always the heroine. Her name was Catherine, but the boys called her "Cathy." She did us a great turn. The dear little thing, unlike most of her sex, was quite punctual—and so were we. We waited and watched and when she went down to the basement, we all trooped after her. Even if we couldn't carry on a conversation with her, no matter; it was grand just to be in the same room with her. We would bustle around, posing, acting, and showing off for her benefit, or merely sit and watch her adoringly. A good time was had by all. Afterwards, this same little Cathy became most famous. Her surname is not mentioned here because she might not care to have those poverty-stricken days recalled.

The actors of that day certainly weren't all celibates. When these same Thespians were glorified by makeup and author's lines they became storybook heroes, particularly to feminine audiences. In these traveling companies there naturally was every sort of character. When work was over some went home to books and studies. Some went home to wives and hubbies. Among the other male members, however, there was usually a Don Juan or two. They had plenty of opportunity to woo droves of ladies, as they generally stayed in one town but a week. In fact, they stayed in each town such a short time that they did not have time to collect bad reputations. In those days, actors weren't supposed to have reputations, anyway.

Each town had its own group of stage-struck maidens. They would wait outside the stage door after each opening performance, and the Casanovas of the company usually had a good selection to pick over. I have seen hundreds of women mobbing a stage door as they waited for a popular matinee idol. They would often fairly rush the poor chap, tearing his buttons off for souvenirs. He generally needed a police escort to get safely through the frantic crowd.

Very often a few durable souls would follow a company to a nearby town, and the Great Lovers had adventures galore with the added assurance that this sort of affair attracted little attention from those not concerned. In this at least they had a decided advantage on the motion picture actor. For example, suppose a Clark Gable, Robert Taylor, or Tyrone Power should elect to play the field, he would find his range of activities limited, indeed. In the first place, he is for all practical purposes sentenced for life to a sprawling country town—Hollywood. In this burg they pull in the sidewalks at eleven o'clock every

65

night. Any male seen on the street after that hour is under suspicion. The inmates of this town are the most lawed against humans in the world.

Motion picture actors are too well known. Every room they enter has a keyhole in the door and a curious eye on the other side. As Don Juans they would have about as much chance as eunuched goldfish in a glass bowl. Wild life in Hollywood, indeed—why it is strongly rumored that the white dove of purity has its home roost right in the center of it.

Talk about a sailor with a sweetheart in every port! There were long trips between seaports, but the stage actor of the old day had a sweetheart in every town with only a short train ride between towns.

Boston was a city beloved by these Balzac adventurers. Hundreds of art and music students came from all over the nation to Boston. Among these were usually some admirers of the stage gentry, plus the local crop of romantic females. The maids in these theatres were often kept busy just carrying notes from feminine admirers to the actors. And it was a common sight to see closed carriages parked near the stage door . . . the blinds drawn. An actor would approach and only a close observer would discover a feminine presence inside as The Great Lover made a quick entrance, closed the carriage door behind him— and away they went.

In St. Louis, a popular matinee idol had made dates one Saturday night with seven different girls. Possibly he was a cautious chap who didn't relish being "stood up." The entire company lived in a cheap hotel that was also an extremely busy one, particularly on Saturday night. All the idol's dates appeared. His cup of plenty was brimming over and he was drowning in the overflow. The fellow was not exactly a Hercules, that legendary hero who had a hundred love affairs in one evening, and the girls were in a fighting mood. He had planted them all over the lobby. The waiting room, dining room, and even nooks in the reading room were decorated with his charming admirers. How he extricated himself from this contretemps, I never learned.

The twin cities of Minneapolis and St. Paul were renowned for their blonde beauties. One of these justly popular Lorelei was nick-named "the Snow Angel," and she stands out as one of the two most beautiful women I have ever seen. She was long limbed, slender, full busted. She had silky blonde hair, an alabaster skin, and great blue eyes shadowed with long cornsilk lashes. Any ordinarily susceptible male who cast a glance on this maiden was generally stopped dead in his tracks.

Walking through the long corridor of the hotel, she moved with a buoyant adolescence . . . her blonde tresses floating . . . one thigh following the other in Salomic undulation . . . full breasts lifted in challenge to all men. She brought a vision of ancient pagan temples of passion . . . temples turreted with oriental gargoyles and with naves cut in the phallic symbol. You could almost see men in the dim temple halls, straining forward, all eyes on a great raised torchlit dais where ancient priestesses postured and posed in attitudes of seduction—spin-ning one's head with heavily perfumed incense and soft, seductive music. Then, through the minor devotees to Love, Ishtar herself ap-pears . . . Ishtar, the goddess of Love, gliding out with slow, alluring gestures, swaying rythmically with the music . . . slim, perfumed hands loosing the silver veil from her luminous body. Men fall to their knees in frenzied admiration, their eyes riveted on the phallic symbol.

Built of such Arabian Nights stuff, the Snow Angel conjured up many such sleep-disturbing dreams for my mates and me.

We had one fellow in our company who was poetically inclined. He was very sensitive about his height, being quite short, and his face resembled that of Edgar Allan Poe. He had been told this latter fact so often that he now dressed the part and recited poetry by the yard. He was forever quoting homemade rhymes that got him nothing but the Bronx cheer from the boys but made quite a hit with the ladies. This was the pet verse that he chanted into feminine ears from Maine to the Golden Gate and usually got results:

"To hold you 'till one stilled you;
"To feed you 'till one filled you;
"To kiss you 'till one killed you:
"Sweet lips, if love could kill."

The scamp slipped this stanza into the shell-pink ear of the Snow Angel and stole her away. He swore later that on this Christmas night she lay on his couch for hours—so beautiful that all he could do was sit and feast his eyes upon her. When he told the gang this, they chorused: "Well, for gossakes, what was the idea?" In ecstatic, dreamy tones, he murmured, "I knew I would never see anything so beautiful as she again. It was enough just to be able to keep that lily in memory forever—unspoiled."

Occasionally into this world a woman appears of such radiant loveliness that this alone is enough to make her fame—the Helens of Troy, the Nanons, the Langtrys. The other beauty referred to was Lady Diana Manners, now the wife of Duff Cooper, who is one of England's political leaders.

In 1917, we were making a propaganda picture for the Allies and were taking scenes on Lady Mary Paget's country place just outside London. In this picture I used a group of women from the noblest families of England. In one scene, Lady Diana was to walk directly towards the camera. She wore a white evening gown of some soft, flowing material and looked "divinely tall and most divinely fair." She was in all actuality the "daughter of a hundred earls" and looked the part. As she approached the camera, walking with exquisite grace, Billy Bitzer, my verteran cameraman who had seen shoals of beautiful women, looked up and saw her for the first time. The vision gave him such a start that his hands began trembling. He forgot to turn the camera and just stared. Lady Diana was asked to repeat the scene, and she complied graciously upon learning the reason.

Once when down to my last dime, I sold the *New York World* a story on Southern cooking for $5. The editor asked for art, so I sent him a photograph of a wooden paving brick covered with grass from Battery Park. The brick was duly published as a "rare Southern dish."

After vainly trying to get a day laborer's job on the Irish-dominated work gangs in New York, I carefully acquired an Irish brogue and was soon happily scraping rust from the iron supports in the new subway for two dollars and twenty-five cents a day. All this time I was living at the theatrical boarding house and, of course, had to keep up a front. What a merciless ribbing I would have received if the actors had seen me costumed as a day laborer. So I would slip out the back way every morning and don my overalls in the alley. Thus, between honest day labor and dishonest scribbling I managed to while the time away.

In the meantime I had discovered that people actually earn a living by writing. I had been writing more or less all my life but had entertained little hope of making any money from it. This business of being a day laborer, however, was also uncertain. Jobs in this line were often as difficult to get as those in the theatre.

In the spring of 1907 I finished a play called *The Fool and the Girl* and sent it to Mr. James K. Hackett, the theatrical producer. Mr. Hackett was then vacationing at his Canadian camp where he was entertaining several New York critics. Later, he told me he had read the play one night to his assembled guests and they had liked it. He sent me a check for $1,000. Afterwards, I wondered if Hackett's guests hadn't been drinking something more potent than Manitoba spring water. Upon receiving the check I was stunned. When finally out of the trance, I rushed pell-mell to the nearest bank—for, by this time, starvation had become not only imminent but an assured fact. And ever since the teller told me that check was good for hard cash, my eyebrows have remained a quarter inch higher than they should be.

One thousand dollars for putting down on paper one word after another! The world was full of words; there were thousands in the dictionaries alone. Believe me, I was going to use them all and get rich quick. A short story was bustled off to *Cosmopolitan*, and Mr. Perriton Maxwell, the editor at that time, paid me three cents a word for each and every word. In short order, Leslie's *Weekly* put $15 in my sinking fund for a scrap of verse called "The Wild Duck." It seemed there was more money in putting down words that didn't rhyme.

Then I engaged in some cerebral pyrotechnics. If one play could make $1,000, ten plays would make $10,000. I started writing on ten plays at once, but before earning this "sure-fire easy money," my play went into rehearsal in Ford's Theatre in Washington. Marc Klaw, of Klaw and Erlanger, lent Fanny Ward for the leading role.

69

Frequently I was ejected into the alley behind the theatre for objecting to changes in the script. Mr. Hackett saw only the last rehearsal and remarked drily, "Well, Griffith, they have certainly done a lot of spoiling of the play I bought—but it's too late now to do anything about it."

The opening night of *The Fool and the Girl* was something to stick in a critic's memory. The perennially youthful Miss Fanny Ward was in the lead as a sixteen-year-old heroine. Briefly, the plot was concerned with a beautiful but giddy heroine. Falling in with a streetwalker and a card sharp, Dumb Dora is set to needling a country bumpkin who had just fallen heir to some important money. She accomplished this by sundry sob routines, at one time extracting no little cash from our innocent young hero by sobbing, "My poor old mother . . . she has the most beautiful eyes in all the world . . . she is very ill and is about to lose her happy"—choke—"happy home." The denouement arrives with the rustic asking our heroine to marry him and the girl too astonished to refuse him. Now she is in a dilemma. She has ranted so much about the love she bears her mother and the beauty of her mother's great big blue eyes that she insists upon her two pals finding a "mother," so that her betrothed will feel all is kosher.

The next scene finds the prostitute indignantly bellowing out over the footlights, "Say! There ain't one single goddam blue-eyed mother in all San Francisco. Belasco has got a pretty good one working for him over at his theatre, but she's got coal-black lamps. I got some damned tramp tied up downstairs, but what a ham! She'll blow our lines in the first act."

Ninety patrons walked out, leaving eleven practically alone. Next morning—September 13, 1907—the Washington critics applied the old blister. One wrote, "If this be art, it is the art of Zola, and Washington wants none of it." Of course, such advertising packed the house for the rest of the week.

Mr. Hackett wanted to make some changes in the cast before trying New York. Klaw and Erlanger refused to allow any juggling with the cast and the show never reached New York, which was doubtless just as well for me. My Washington experience had worried off exactly thirty-three pounds. Had the show gone to New York, the astute critics there—those acid-throwers—doubtless would have blistered the rest of my poundage off and that would have been the end of me. Anyhow, *The Fool and the Girl* was said to have been the first "damn—damn" American drama.

Mr. Hackett went stony broke, but later inherited several millions and went abroad to dazzle England with a series of lavish productions.

Part Three

WHEN I LANDED in New York shortly after the Washington fiasco, the very first thing I met was—The Old Wolf. We walked familiarly together down Fourteenth Street where I witnessed my first motion picture in a nickelodeon. The only impressive thing about it was the long queue waiting outside to buy tickets.

A few days later I was talking to a skinny actor named Salter. He had a funereal face that looked like it had worn out eight bodies. The boys called him "Gloomy Gus." We were at a table in a dark corner of Three-Cent John's Eating Emporium and Gloomy Gus remarked, "Why don't you try the Biograph picture studio—that Fourteenth Street joint?"

"Do you think I'd stand a chance?" I replied.

Gloomy Gus leaned forward, at the same time lifting his left hand over one eye—doubtless to eclipse the grinning wolf sitting there between us—and said, "Well, there's no harm trying. You might even sell them a scenario."

Losing no time, I bundled up an armful of hurriedly written scenarios and, accompanied by my furry shadow, hustled over to Walter McCutcheon, the Biograph director. I condescendingly informed Mr. McCutcheon that I was willing to lend my great talents as an actor to his company. He didn't seem overwhelmed by my generosity but took my name and said he would "let you know if anything turned up."

He also took the scenarios and placed them on his desk—dangerously near the wastepaper basket, I thought. But those stories were good, I knew, most of them having been borrowed from the very best authors. After receiving his promise to look them over, I departed. Afterwards, I did manage to pick up a five-dollar bill occasionally, knocking out ham scenarios.

A great wave of reform was sweeping the countryside at this time. Newspapers were laying down a barrage against gambling, rum, and light ladies, particularly the light ladies. You could tell how sincere the papers were by the way they worked from the ground up, emblazoning pictures of the light ladies' hosiery all over their front pages. There were campaigns against everything. So I decided to help reform the motion picture business. This latter industry was in such low state that it paid the best Roman-nosed actor only $5 a day, and a like sum for immortal scenarios. If I could only lift this art up to where it would pay me a regular salary each and every week!

In June of that year [1908], Arthur Marvin suggested to his brother, H. M. Marvin, president of the Biograph Company, that I be made an assistant director. A few weeks later I directed my first picture, *The Adventures of Dollie*, an epic that was made in two days at a cost of $65.

Whenever I read now of the millionaire leading men and women of today, when I see statements of their income taxes running into hundreds of thousands of dollars, I am very much impressed with the difference between conditions now and those of twenty-six years ago in the motion picture business.

We were making "colossal" feature pictures in 1909 and '10. They ran about six or seven minutes on the screen and their cost averaged—not millions as now—but about $150. There were some stories that I wanted to make into pictures, and I needed a good leading man. Not being satisfied with the few who happened to drop in, I took a trip up Broadway and strolled around in front of the agencies . . . afraid to go inside. Any regular legitimate agency would have thrown me out.

Finally, a chap came out of one of these agencies, and it seemed to me, at first glance, that he was just the man. He was over six feet tall, dark, had slightly wavy hair, pale complexion, classical features, and the air of a gentleman. So I tagged after him, screwing up enough courage to approach him.

After begging his pardon, I asked, "Do you happen to be an actor?"

He gazed at me quizzically, then drawled, "Well, that is a moot point. Some say 'yes,' but most say 'no.' "

Apologetically, I told him that I was a motion picture director. There was considerable hesitation on my part before this painful fact was dragged out into the public light, knowing only too well the great contempt in which movies were held then by stage people. So I quickly added, "But the pictures we're making are different." My prospective victim purred, "Judging by the ones I've seen, it would seem a good idea to make them different."

In common with all our tribe devoted solely to art, he asked, "How much?" When told we were paying only $5 a day now, but hoped soon to be able to raise the ante, he asked coldly, "Cash?" I replied, "So far —at the end of each and every day." Then he confessed to a continued interest in eating daily, and we finally arranged for him to start the next day. His name was Arthur Johnson. A wardrobe? Johnson replied, "Certainly, I've got it on." He was assured that this wardrobe would be all right for this next picture and that he would have two whole days' work, maybe three.

Three days was all the time we were allowed for the making of any picture. This included writing the story, preparation—everything. The wardrobe Johnson boasted was a dark blue suit, slightly shiny but well pressed, and, as he had broad shoulders and a slim, wedge-shaped figure, it passed inspection. This one-suit wardrobe of Arthur's became the most photographed suit the world has ever seen. He wore it in at least twenty pictures. Later, when we suggested that he get another suit, he seemed slightly indignant, drawling, "What's the matter with this one? It has always been all right in the past."

Arthur Johnson had a great personality. He merely had to put in an appearance in any sort of assemblage and most everybody warmed to him. Incidentally, he was the son of an Episcopalian minister and quite well educated. He was one of two people in my employ who actually refused a salary raise.

The other chap was a philosophical Russian Jew, Abraham Schultz. He had the same charming, abstract smile as Johnson and was a valuable man in our darkroom. The cameramen were always squabbling with the darkroom men. "You ruined the film developing it," one would say. "That's your fault—your exposure was lousy," would be the retort. One was always blaming it on the other, and neither would ever admit that he was wrong. But not Schultz.

One day after looking at a very poor shot on the screen, I asked Schultz what was wrong. Instead of blaming it on the cameraman, Schultz replied, "Well, Mr. Griffith, I suppose I left it in the bath a little too long and it's overdeveloped. I went over the film carefully and the exposure seems all right. I'll try to make a better print."

This attitude was so rare and also so valuable that Schultz stayed with the company as long as the writer did.

When the company became more prosperous, I said to Schultz one day, "We are going to give you a raise. Everybody else is getting one and we are going to give you one, too." He replied casually, "I don't think I would do that, Mr. Griffith. I am getting all the money I need. Don't bother." But Schultz got the raise, and afterwards I received hearty thanks from several members of the Russian colony (nearly all the men working in our laboratory belonged to this colony) for Schultz's raise. He had given it to them. It is said that Trotzky was aided by this same colony at one time.

Arthur Johnson made a similar refusal of a raise. This occurred behind several mugs of beer at Luchow's famous place on Fourteenth Street in New York. I made quite a flourish in telling Arthur that we were giving him a raise. After some little thought, he said, "Well, I don't know about that. I don't think that's such a hot idea. I am making just about enough to provide me all I need to eat and drink, and if I get more money I might do more of both than would be good for me. Maybe you had better let it stay as it is." But Arthur, also, got his raise—and afterwards was stolen away from Biograph by the Lubin Company and given what was considered in that day a really big salary.

About art, no matter what anybody says, believe me, a lot of it has gotten into motion pictures since my beginning. To me, however, art in those days merely meant Johnson's given name.

When I finally was working at a more or less steady job as a director with the old Biograph Company, my bosses saw to it that neither my name nor that of any actor ever became known to the public. The leading people in these pictures were known merely as a Biograph man or Biograph girl.

The last Biograph girl was getting difficult. She wanted more than $15 for a three-day week. So while the movie industry was in upheaval over this horrible state of affairs, a boy who ran errands and helped around what we laughingly called the prop department, stopped chewing gum long enough to inform me that a young lady wanted to see me out in the hall. We were using the hall of an old brownstone house for a general office. The boy paused, then added, "—a good-looker."

After carefully trimming the saw-tooth edges off my collar, I assumed a debonair manner and sauntered out to meet the young lady.

In rapid fire, she informed me that she was a regular actress and had been the last season with Mr. David Belasco, but would condescend to work for a short period in the movies. While she was talking I took stock of my visitor. Besides standard parts, she had a small, cute figure . . . golden curls . . . creamy complexion . . . sparkling Irish eyes—eyes with languorous capabilities. Even in that day of reformers this particular young lady did not seem in need of any reforming.

"Well, Miss——"

"Miss Pickford is the name—Mary Pickford."

"Well, Miss Pickford, I think you'll do. We'll take you on trial and guarantee three days' work each week at $5 a day, and if we should need you more often, we'll pay $5 for each extra day."

"Well, Mr. Griffit——"

"The name is Griffith."

"Well, Mr. Griffith, you must realize that I'm an actress. I have had important parts with Mr. Belasco on the *real* stage. I'm an actress and an artist and I must have a guarantee of $25 a week and extra when I work extra."

Boy! When that little girl talked up that twenty-five bucks, her eyes fairly gleamed. You could see *art* sparkling all over her. We were going to have a conference, tomorrow, I said, and her proposition would be submitted to the board. You might say that this was the beginning of art in the movies.

The result of our conference was that Miss Pickford was hired on her own terms. It certainly is remarkable when we pause to reflect that art "for art's sake alone" from that time on has been rushing headlong into the movies.

Mary's Irish rose one day, and she told me in no uncertain terms that—no matter what we thought—one day she would be earning $100 a week. Four years later, she was making $10,000 a week.

Mary had her troubles, too. The bosses, after seeing her on the screen in a couple of pictures, told me to fire her—"her head is too big for her body." This made me take inventory of Mary again, and I saw that there was some truth in their statement but figured the stuff she had inside her head would more than make up for this small deficiency. It took quite some argument to convince the bosses that they should keep her on the payroll.

Mary deserves her reputation of possessing rare business acumen, and more power to her. She has given away fortunes, however, particularly to her relatives, for Mary was always intensely loyal to her family.

Mack Sennett, famous director of comedies, was brought to me, like Mary Pickford, by Bobby Harron, the boy-of-all-trades around the Biograph studio. Bobby came into my office early one morning and confided that "a strong man wants to see you outside." Just what he meant by "strong" I wasn't sure until he explained that the visitor was a vaudeville strong man, weightlifter, etc. I asked Bobby where he was. He replied, "Why, he's out on the sidewalk."

"Why doesn't he come inside?"

"Well, I guess from the way he talked," answered Bobby thoughtfully, "he has been asked out of so many places like this that he just thought he would save himself the trouble and annoyance this time by staying out until he found which way the wind blew."

So I journeyed out to the sidewalk, and soon afterward Mack Sennett became Biograph's principal slapstick comedian.

Mack played the leading role in one of the first wild slapstick comedies under my direction. It was one of those freewheeling comedies, and he was supposed during the action of the picture to carry home a curtain pole, stopping to quaff a flock of drinks on the way. Next, he good naturedly invites the driver of the hansom cab to join him. After taking on quite a cargo, they start for home, Mack inside the cab with the curtain pole sticking out the windows on both sides. They take a wild, zigzag course with the ends of the curtain pole becoming variously entangled with market carts, baby carriages, etc., leaving in their wake a long trail of rough, slapstick gags—all to the vest-disturbing delight of the audiences of that day. Of course, this was the same Mack Sennett who became famous for his bathing beauty comedies.

Arthur Johnson and Sennett became inseparable pals. The pair presented a study in contrast. Johnson was tall, debonair, possessing the easy manner of the aristocrat. Sennett had a short, burly, bearlike figure with long gorilla arms dropping from a pair of incredibly huge shoulders. And always there was a wide, good-natured grin on his face. Sennett adored Johnson, and they used to put on a very hilarious sketch. Entering a hotel lobby, barroom, or restaurant, Johnson would lead Sennett in by the hand, introducing him right and left with great gravity as "my idiot brother." He would refuse to let Mack have liquor, food, etc., telling many long-winded ridiculous stories about the actions of his "idiot brother"; how he got that way, etc. Mack would act the part to the best of his ability while Arthur looked on with an "understanding" smile on his handsome face. They took great delight in making asses of themselves, and a good time was had by all.

In the old Biograph studio we had one small room set apart for the men's dressing room. Between scenes the actors would spend most of their time there, shooting craps. Called on a set, they would drop the dice, rush out, go through the scene—and then back to the dice.

There was a big ex-wrestler named Williams. He weighed about two hundred and fifty pounds and, from the neck down, was strong as

79

an ox. Apparently, he had only two loves in his life—dice and Lionel Barrymore.

Lionel Barrymore came to Biograph in 1910, about the same time Williams did. Some years before this Lionel had been a hit on Broadway in a company headed by his uncle, John Drew. He left the stage to become a painter and had several pictures hung in the Paris salons. He proclaimed the artist's life as "the most glorious in the world—with one slight exception—you didn't eat."

Lionel Barrymore, besides being a great actor, is a brilliant conversationalist and can talk learnedly on most any subject and spice that talk with a dry, subtle wit. He would come around every morning and ask if we didn't want a fine actor to play a policeman, asserting that he could play a policeman better than any human being. In his now-famous drawl, he would add that if there weren't any policeman parts open, he was good in any kind of role—so long as he got the necessary five bucks. At that time Lionel was quite an athlete and a great admirer of physical prowess. He would slyly try to lead Williams into conversation, trying to find out what in the world was going on in Williams' mind, if anything.

Lionel Barrymore and [I] held a reunion two years ago [1937?] at the Academy of Motion Picture Arts and Sciences' dinner. We hadn't seen each other in years. His first question was: "Do you ever see anything of Williams any more?"

Several of these old-time movie actors lived in the same old lodging house in which I had lived as a stage actor, and I sometimes visited Johnson and Sennett there. These two, however, were somewhat better off than I had been. They even had soup for dinner. One night in the old lodging house Johnson and Sennett were pulling one of the clown acts with Johnson drawling dogmatically, "The partaking of soup is a mighty affair, Mr. Sennett. Never, never should one annoy one's neighbors by unholy sounds when slipping the soup to one's lips. Do not take it from the bowl like that! Among the elect they use a spoon. Didn't you ever hear of that?"

"Well, I *am* using a spoon, ain't I?"

"Yes, dear fellow, but only after my reprimand. Now take the spoon—thus—hold it close to your manly bosom, gently clasped by the ends of the digits. Now—without undue haste—push the spoon away from you, and into the soup. Describe a graceful arc and return it to your lips—and let this entire act be accompanied with silence."

"What do you mean?" Mack would sputter. "That's a goofy idea. If you want to bring the soup to you—why push it away first?"

"Be not indignant, young man, I mean all for the best. If you would earn the admiration of the epicurean world . . . that is, if you should be allowed by chance into some first-class restaurant . . . you must pursue the etiquette I have outlined for you."

Dear old Mack Sennett, when he actually did start making a little money, reserved a table in the window of Jack's restaurant, famous rendezvous of actors, writers, prizefighters, and celebrities from every walk of life. No inhabitant of this old theatrical boarding house had ever had enough money at one time to even dare think of entering Jack's. And Mack Sennett let it be known to one and all in this lodging house, and the adjoining one as well, that he intended to dine at eight that night at the best table in Jack's place. Not a few actually strolled by the restaurant to watch Sennett eat in a first-class New York cafe. And did Mack sit back and bask in the reflected shine of all that gleaming napery and cutlery! While waiters bobbed around him, he partook of every course from soup to nuts. Solomon in all his glory was not so grand as he.

Photography at this stage of the game was very crude. The bosses had told me that you must have the sun over your shoulders as you stood by the camera in order that the light would fall directly on the faces of the actors. All scenes had to be photographed in this manner and the most beautiful girl in the world, photographed this way, would have gotten a raw deal. In nature, I would see lovely pastoral scenes with the light coming from behind. This was how I wanted to photograph scenes for my pictures. The cameraman said, "It may look good to *your* eye, but it won't look so good in the finished picture. The actors' faces will be black."

Not believing the cameramen, I sneaked a camera out one Sunday, paid for the film, and made a picture. This film was run off secretly

81

after development, and I discovered that the cameramen were right—the faces were black as coal.

One day in Fort Lee, New Jersey, we were preparing to dine in the backyard of a cheap Italian restaurant when the waiter threw a white tablecloth over the table. The actors were sitting across from me, backlighted by the sun which was giving a soft glow to the landscape. But the actors' faces were lighted, too! The tablecloth had served as a reflector. Taking another chance, I promptly photographed several scenes using a white bedsheet for a reflector. When they were projected on the screen, I thought them beautiful, but the studio heads squawked, "You've got to cut that out. It's terrible. Why, it isn't even in focus and, besides, it's too dim."

It so happened that Mr. J. J. Kennedy, vice president of the Empire State Trust Company and holder of the dough-bag for our company, collected steel engravings as a hobby, and when he saw these scenes, exclaimed: "Why, they look like steel engravings! Stick to that idea!" And we did. So the Jersey Italian's tablecloth became the papa of all modern studio lighting.

In the days when the motion picture industry was but a lusty infant, most everyone got into the business more by accident than design. Today, however, when someone becomes famous for hopping the ocean or piling matches on a beer bottle top, all the producing companies are after him, bidding wildly against each other in the race to get this particular person on their own payroll. But not in the old days.

One day in the early summer of 1909 I was going through the dingy old hall of the Biograph studio when suddenly all the gloom seemed to disappear. The change was caused by the presence of two young girls sitting side by side on a hall bench. They were blonde and fair and sitting affectionately close together. Certainly, I had never seen a prettier picture. Both were explaining to Bobby Harron that they were waiting for Miss Pickford, "—we were child actresses together."

They were Lillian and Dorothy Gish. Of the two, Lillian shone with an exquisitely fragile, ethereal beauty.

Only recently Alexander Woollcott commented in print on Lillian's Camille—"But in the death-bed scene there was around Miss Gish a strange, mystic light that was not made by any electrician." And when I first saw her sitting there in that dingy old hall, there seemed around her a luminous glow that did not come from the skylight.

As for Dorothy, she was lovely, too, but in another manner—pert, saucy, the old mischief popping out of her. Yet, she had a certain tender charm. Dorothy was forever teasing Lillian, poking fun at her. Even when they were very young, Dorothy called her sister "Old Lil."

The Gish family, which included the two girls and their mother, were highly devoted to each other. To the cynical this might read like the droolings of a press agent, but once when Mrs. Gish was stricken ill, the sisters spent a fortune on her in an attempt to recoup her health, carrying her to every country in Europe to visit the great specialists. For months they gave up everything else in trying to save her.

Lillian had been a child actress with Mary Pickford in the old days. Then the family sent her to a convent where she stayed several years. Now, she was attempting a return to the stage. Both the Gish girls played only a few parts with me that summer, and then Lillian joined a Belasco company. She stayed with this show for some time. In the meanwhile, Biograph moved to California. During the summer and early winter we would now make pictures in New York, moving to California for the rest of the year for the steady sunshine and changes of locale.

Miss Lillian, always delicate, became seriously ill during our first California winter, and the kind Belasco paid her expenses to the Golden State for the sake of her health. It was thought at this time that she had but a short time to live. With her mother's care and an outdoor life, however, she improved rapidly and soon was made a regular member of the Biograph Company.

Another member of our company at this time was Blanche Sweet. This actress' beauty was of the voluptuous, glamorous type, and she had real ability. She was a sensational success playing opposite Henry Walthall in *Judith of Bethulia* [1914], Biograph's first long picture. We

83

took two whole weeks to make this picture, spending more than $13,000 in my extravagance and getting in Dutch with the bosses again.

When working in New York we frequently went out to a village called Cuddiebackville for exterior shots. It was quite a photogenic spot, this green valley set between the mountains. An old tourist hotel was there and a lake with a picturesque canal that led to a river. It was a grand locale for Indian pictures, and the members of the company, when idle, would disport themselves swimming, canoeing, etc. Not infrequently on moonlit nights the cause of romance progressed.

Actors who were fearful-looking warriors by day sang love songs by night. The canoes, useful during working hours for The Chase, had a gentler job by night, carrying lovers. Among these twosomes was one particular couple. They made a grand picture together—Mary Pickford and Owen Moore.

We always took someone on location who could play the piano so we could dance in the evening. Nearly the entire company was composed of youngsters, and we worked and played with the buoyant spirit of youth. We were young like the business itself . . . happy-go-lucky, vigorous, vital, crude, lusty.

It was here at Cuddiebackville that the first "fade" or blackout was used. Pictures formerly came to a sudden stop at the end of every scene. This always annoyed me, so one day I tried an experiment. Taking a cigar box, I had it placed in front of the camera lens. The lid of the box was lifted gradually before the lens so that when the scene was projected on the screen, instead of that sudden stop—it faded off. The picture in which this effect was first used was *The Last of the Mohicans*, starring Mary Pickford and Owen Moore.

Later we had a metal iris made by the local blacksmith in Cuddiebackville and discarded the cigar box. Some of the studio heads did not like this effect, either, complaining that it used up extra film. But the idea was soon generally adopted, and the dissolve is used today in every picture. Had I had any common sense at all and had these ideas patented, they would be worth millions to me today.

By this time Biograph had become the most famous motion picture company in the world. Its stock, which had been absolutely worthless a few years before, now soared. Powerful Biograph now forced a combination with the Edison Company and was sued in 1913 by the United States Government under the trust laws. The government figures proved that on a capitalization of several million dollars, Biograph had earned *seventeen hundred percent profit* in one year alone. Wouldn't any of the big producing companies today like to earn a fraction of that percentage!

Being too busy working day and night in making the pictures, I knew nothing of all this prosperity going on over my head. They were now giving me $50 a week, and I was scared each and every day that I would lose my job. The officials at the Fourteenth Street office would frequently telephone to Cuddiebackville about various matters concerning the film. My most vivid memory of that beautiful place is going to the telephone with my heart in my mouth, in fear of the fatal news—I was fired again. Great was my relief when the New York office began talking about the exposure we were using or some other minor matter.

The "close-up," however, preceded Cuddiebackville. The first pictures closely imitated stage technique. The characters came on, did their bits, and went off, exactly as they do on the stage. In *The Adventures of Dollie,* my first effort, we used the technique that is practically the same as is used today. This is now called parallel action. And it is this switching from one scene to another that gives the motion picture its breadth, speed, and variety. The bosses told me to shoot the pictures so as to get full-sized figures. These full figures, however, appeared so distant on the screen that the audience could not see the actors' expressions. So I dared to make a close view—just their faces. It is now called the "close-up."

Billy Bitzer, famous cameraman of that day, refused to take this kind of picture. He said it would throw the background out of focus. This was a puzzler. So I journeyed up to the Metropolitan Museum of Art and spent quite some time studying the works of great painters. Rembrandt and other painters backed me up. All painted pictures showing only the face.

85

Managing to get another cameraman, we photographed the close-up. But when the audience in one of the first nickelodeons saw these pictures, they howled their disapproval. They wanted to know "what the devil" had happend to the actors' feet. This innovation, however, was soon in general use. I must confess that I have seen some close-ups—particularly when they disclose a performer's tonsils—that made me wish I hadn't been so smart. It has been said that close-ups had been made before this time. If so, they were not in use, and neither I nor my company ever saw or heard of them.

Things started popping now. The movie baby was getting growing pains. It was getting to be quite a husky youngster—crude, raucous, vigorous. The Motion Picture Patents company, of which Biograph was the head, lost its patent suits. It had held patents on production and exhibition of pictures. They had made every exhibitor kick in so much a week just for the right to run pictures. Now the combine was broken. Anybody could make pictures. New talent, new brains jumped in.

We were receiving splendid pictures from France about this time. The best actors in France from the Comédie Française worked in these pictures, while in America an actor of reputation would not dare to be seen in one. Thus, these foreign pictures were giving us real competition.

Then Adolph Zukor appeared on the scene. He liked to come over and watch us make pictures. He, too, decided to form a company and get in The Gold Rush. Zukor had imagination and worlds of energy. His enthusiasm filled the air like an electrical storm.

William Fox began to literally throw pictures at the public—melodramas, down-to-earth stories. Theda Bara was giving dreams to prosaic housewives. Samuel Goldwyn leaped into the fray. Don't let anybody kid you about Mr. Goldwyn. He also had plenty of imagination. He was a hot dynamo with ideas to burn. I have seen him work, painstaking to the nth degree. They say he lost many millions learning the game, but he did learn it and is today one of the few who knows his business.

Jessy Lasky had found success on the stage and in vaudeville, etc.

His "Three Rosebuds" act was famous. Now he swung into the great movies. He was one of the best supervisors ever in the business. Given the right chance, he'd show them.

Before the beginning of The Gold Rush I had made the first picture to run over one thousand feet in length. It was called *His Trust*. The combine limited everyone to one thousand feet. This picture ran two thousand feet. Getting my dander up, I fought the cutters and they compromised by making it a serial. So *His Trust*, at one thousand feet, was featured one week. The next week *His Trust* was *Fulfilled*. Now anyone could see that longer pictures were on the way.

My *Judith of Bethulia* ran four thousand feet—four reels. Two weeks was allowed me for the making of two special features. We tossed off a quickie in one day, leaving me thirteen days for *Judith*. I thought *Judith* was an epic. The bosses rather liked it too, but they thought it cost too much money—$13,000.

Soon Biograph began expanding. They made an arrangement with Klaw & Erlanger and the tycoons who controlled the regular theatre to get their best stage plays. They built a million-dollar studio on 186th Street and scrapped the old Fourteenth Street dump. They procured real stage-play directors. Since I was only a movie man, they would let me supervise, but not direct any more. *Judith* had double-crossed me. She had cost too much money and the company, I knew, was reaching for the ax.

In the little park before the studio there jutted a large rock. At odd times I would sit on this rock and try to peer into the future, but all I could see was a mass of gloom. I thought I knew an exit cue when I heard one, and here it came. One day summoning all the nerve I could muster, I bolted into the office of Mr. Kennedy, the president. I asked for more authority and a percentage of the profits—or else. I rather suspect now that he was "tickled pink" at my demands. He really was quite a gentleman, and I believe he actually disliked to use the ax himself, but now that I had brought it out for him, he let it fall. He told me "Griffith, you are only a small cog in the big wheel, as I, myself, am—and any of the cogs can be spared." So I "got the works." I left the Biograph Studio in great despair, and "so help me God," there in the side yard sitting up, licking his chops, looking right at me, was an enormous wolf. On closer inspection he proved to be just an actor working in an animal picture.

Among the new groups coming into the motion picture business was one headed by Harry Aitken and some friends. They were a pretty smart crowd and had everything to insure success, except money. We got together and managed to rake up just about enough cash to make one cheap picture, with a young author, Dr. Goodman. We worked out an idea together for a movie story. Next, we rented a cheap hall on Sixteenth Street and Broadway, and cleared the decks for action.

We called this six-reel opus the *Battle of the Sexes,* and worked day and night to finish it in five days. The fifth day was the deadline and that was as far as the money would go. In the old bromidic triangle, Lillian Gish and Bobby Harron, the ex-prop boy, played the juvenile leads. Luck was with us. It made a hit. We made others.

Our new company was called The Mutual. Remember the slogan—"The Mutual Pictures Make Time Fly"? It was "mutual" all right. I did the work, and they got the profits. In succession we made *Macbeth, Don Quixote,* Poe's *Tell-Tale Heart,* Kingsley's *Sands of Dee.* We even had poetry in the screen titles. We also produced *Blot on the Escutcheon* and *Pippa Passes* from the difficult Robert Browning. A widely known producer today once wrote to "Mr. Robert Browning," care of our studios, and asked if he had any peppy, up-to-date stories or comedies. I wrote him right back. We had quite a correspondence.

It was around this time that one of the first motion picture critics, Frank Woods, came into the company. One fortunate day he brought a book in to me. It was *The Clansman* by Thomas Dixon. I skipped quickly through the book until I got to the part about the Klansmen, who, according to no less than Woodrow Wilson, ran to the rescue of the downtrodden South after the Civil War. I could just see these Klansmen in a movie with their white robes flying.

We had had all sorts of runs-to-the-rescue in pictures and horse operas. The old United States Cavalry would gallop to the rescue— East, one week; West, the next. It was always a hit. The-pursuit-and-run-to-the-rescue seemed to be the most surefire gag in the business.

The great Walter Disney seems to believe in this today. If you analyze his cartoons, invariably they contain this motion picture technique.

Now I could see a chance to do this ride-to-the-rescue on a grand scale. Instead of saving one poor little Nell of the Plains, this ride would be to save a nation. Here was a chance to make a moving picture that would rival the productions of the regular stage. It would take two and half hours in its showing. Forgetting the pain in my neck from the ax wielded by Biograph, I started to work up enthusiasm with my associates. This was too easy. Just like that everything was set —but "where in the hell" were we going to get the money? We looked into the dough bag, and it was practically empty, at least as far as making a picture of this magnitude was concerned.

Mr. Dixon wanted $10,000 for the story—cash. We painted red-hot pictures of ten times that much rolling in in royalties. "Just think—just think, Mr. Dixon, *we will let you have twenty-five percent of the profits.*" We painted a glorious future of actually paying thousands out to him, when Mr. Dixon interrupted with that bromide about, "A bird in the hand—." We filled the air with clouds of pity at such short-sighted ideas. We "built" him a grand house on Fifth Avenue; had the food, wine, and servants all installed out of these golden royalties, when he crackled, in a chilly December voice, "I've heard something about movie royalties. They sound nice, but nobody ever gets them."

The charming Mr. Dixon clouded our lives for months and all over this piece of small change—$10,000. We couldn't go anywhere but what the estimable Mr. Dixon would pop up before us, asking, "When do I get the $10,000?" We never gave it to him for an excellent reason. We didn't have it to give.

The Clansman had been a terrible frost as a stage play and they had made a movie of it which did not get over even in the South, so we didn't blame Mr. Dixon for wanting the $10,000 in advance.

The royalties finally agreed on paid him more than a million dollars. But I am quite sure Mr. Dixon wasn't any more surprised at this outcome than we were ourselves.

The Epoch crowd agreed to put up the unheard-of sum of $100,000 to make the picture. They had to get this money by selling stock.

At last, we got started. We were going to spend $100,000 to make one motion picture—a "gawd-awful" sum in that day. The most expensive theatrical entertainment, we thought, since Caesar had plated the arena in Rome with silver as a part of a magnificent pageant. Caesar, nearing middle age, was being called a useless drunken wastrel. Sick with envy of the military triumphs of Pompey the Great, he spent his all and dazzled Rome with a colossal farewell party. The show made such a hit with the populace that it started him on his way to glory.

In our small way, we hoped to be lucky, too. We gathered a cast together. Henry Walthall had been with me for a year. Walthall had a patrician's face—coal-black hair waving off a splendid forehead. He was ideal for the lead, but this character was to epitomize all the heroes of The Lost Cause. We all wanted a man at least six feet tall with a powerful physique that would tower magnificently in the old gray uniform, and Walthall was only about five feet six.

We searched and searched, but couldn't discover our ideal. Then— an idea! Napoleon was small. So were other great leaders. We would call Walthall the Little Colonel, put this in the title, and so disarm the audience.

Lillian Gish for the Northern girl and for the Southern feminine lead—who? This character needed an actress who could run the gamut from comedy to the height of tragedy. She should also have the beauty commonly associated with Southern women. We imagined one with great dark eyes, tall, patrician; hair like the sultry Southern night that wears the moon for a gardenia. Again, we searched—and got nowhere.

In our company there was a little freckled-faced girl with blue eyes and hair of indeterminate color. She had come to the studio thinking she might substitute as an extra girl for her sister who was ill. She had played some parts with us and, despite the elusive quality of her personality, had dynamic power. We rehearsed her in the part. No doubt she could play it. Well, all right, she was cast for the part. After she had been on the screen for a few minutes, the audience forgot the color of her hair and eyes. But they remembered her name—Mae Marsh. Sir James M. Barrie once told me that he considered her as fine an actress, if not the finest, as any he had ever seen on stage or screen.

Now that the casting was done, we began rehearsals. A small hall was make-up room for extras in a makeshift building of cheap rough pine. We had hard kitchen chairs. (I never wanted an easy chair on a set. You were apt to get too comfortable and lean back, instead of keeping busy.) We wrote no script. I never did for any of my pictures. We would get the idea of the story, carry it around with us; eat over it; walk over it; drink over it; dream over it until every action and scene was catalogued in our minds. Then we would start rehearsing.

We rehearsed *The Birth of a Nation* two months before we started shooting. (This did not cost much as no one was getting an important salary.) Each actor knew thoroughly every scene he was to play, and there were four thousand separate scenes in *The Birth of a Nation*, some, however, being only a flash of two seconds. This little group in the cheap hall rehearsed for hours and hours, the little group who was to win vivid fame in every country in the world, among millions who had never heard of the United States. The film was shown by traveling companies in the savage wilds of such countries as Borneo, Java, Africa, India, China, etc.

In common with many others, I may poke a little fun at the motion picture business, but it is an institution of tremendous power—the one voice that speaks to the entire world, and in my heart, I really am deeply grateful for the lucky break that allowed me to become a part of the motion picture business.

Finally, the financing company, after sending me a little over half of the amount needed to make the picture, laid an egg. I would be out on the lot all day with a megaphone, shouting to the mob in no uncertain terms just what to do, when raucous voices would reply, "Now we'll tell *you* what to do. Pay us our dough!" We kept going as best we could, hoping daily, hourly, to receive a life-saving check from New York. We could keep the mob in hand in the day. At night, I would escape through the bushes to my hotel to ward off the angry mob. My feet went swiftly, for The Wolf was snapping at my heels.

An idea came to me. I would get the rest of the money in Los Angeles! So at night, after work was over, I pursued every prosperous-looking citizen who came my way in that unfortunate city.

It was being rumored everywhere that even if the picture was finished, it would never be allowed to show in the North. This gossip greatly frightened prospective investors.

There was one native son, a wary citizen, as well he might be. He had scars all over him from having been nicked by various wildcat promotors. He said he might put in $100, but he "knew you wouldn't take such a small sum." Little did he wot. I quickly relieved him before he changed his mind and gave him his one share—one of the most beautiful certificates ever printed.

My big game, however, was Mr. William Clune. He was managing the Los Angeles Auditorium where he had turned a civic enterprise into a motion picture theatre. He didn't think much of the movies, but he was all wrapped up in his orchestra. He had the biggest one in Los Angeles and bragged about it day and night. He advertised his orchestra in the newspapers, instead of his pictures. He was a shrewd businessman by day, but at night he liked relaxation and a little drink now and then. I pursued this poor man into his office nightly. I had two bottles with me. One was whiskey, the other, a liquid made of burnt-sugar water.

After we engaged in conversation I would take a spot with him of the real whiskey—then push the McCoy over to him and drink from the phony whiskey bottle. Being a Kentuckian, I was not rabid against liquor. One cannot stay up until twelve or one o'clock at night imbiding—painting pictures to Mr. Clune about how much money he was going to make—and be on the set before daylight the next morning to battle the salaryless mob.

Finally, after much sweat, I got Mr. Clune out to the studio. We wanted $15,000 from him. Fifteen thousand! With that much we could somehow get through the picture. Mr. Clune walked into the projection room. We got the best projection boy on the lot and warned him, "Be sure to get a good light on that picture." We warned the actors, "Get those sour looks off your faces. Try to look like you get your salary every week."

Mr. Clune saw the rushes, but wasn't impressed. Again gloom stalked the lot. As we came from the projection room to the lot, my assistant was rehearsing the mob, costumed as Confederate soldiers. They were supposed to be a large army marching to war. We had planted a wall on one side and set the camera at an angle. That would deceive the audience. These soldiers were swinging gallantly along in the camera's view. As soon as they got out of the lens' range, they ran behind the wall and came back on again. On the screen it would look like the whole Confederacy on the march.

We had picked up a cheap band which, I am afraid, my assistant had deceived. They didn't know we weren't paying salaries. It was about the "corniest" outfit ever gathered together, but as they approached Mr. Clune, they were playing "Dixie"—an air that is hard to kill. Over the marblelike coldness of his face, came the faint suggestion of a smile. Hope started beating its white wings again. He said in his Western drawl, "Say, that war music would sound great in my theatre with *my* orchestra playing it." As a part of the bait, we had told him he could have the picture in his theatre. If he had only known it, he could have had it for all the West.

Again I soared—"Can you imagine, Mr. Clune, just picture those soldiers marching to the thrilling music of the best orchestra, not only in Los Angeles, but the best in the world—playing Dixie—Dixie! Why you would tear them right out of their chairs." He said, "Well, I don't know. Fifteen thousand dollars is a lot of money." "Why Mr. Clune, $15,000 to you is nothing." "Oh yeah! well, it's quite a sum." He hesitated—then continued in a meditative voice, "But in my theatre—with *my* orchestra playing it. Well, no doubt I'll be sorry for it—but all right, I'll let you have it." With one tremendous leap I started for the checkbook. Fortunately, I was behind Mr. Clune and he didn't notice this bit of acrobatics which gave me time to assume an unconcerned manner as we went towards the office. Preceding my victim into the small lair, I managed surreptitiously to whisper to Mr. Epping, the cashier, "For God's sake!—smile! and get the check ready."

Mr. Clune sat down to the desk. Mr. Epping brought the check out and laid it on the desk for his signature. In the meantime we had a little refreshment. This time no burnt sugar for me. The checkbook was gently pushed over to Mr. Clune, and I assumed the old nonchalance and said, "Well, after all, Mr. Clune, I don't want to rush you into this. There is another man over in Pasadena—he doesn't want to go in quite as much as this, but he is good for $12,000." You could hear the clock tick as Mr. Clune's expression took on a tinge of benevolence towards this other investor. We could almost hear him again, "Well, perhaps you had better let him have it."

At long last, he took the pen in hand. Talk about slow moving pictures! How could anyone take so long to sign his name? Finally the heroic deed was done, and we were saved. William Clune made hundreds of thousands out of it.

Several of the workmen who had been with me a long time wanted to invest a few hundred dollars in the picture. The Gishes also had banked about $300 and, despite the fact that it was all they had in the world, wanted to put it in. God bless them! Knowing that all pictures are a gamble, I was afraid to let these good people take a chance and lose their little-all, but afterwards, every time they heard about the enormous returns the investors were receiving, their serio-comic moans could be heard for blocks. I haven't heard the end of it to this day.

Finally the picture was finished, all fourteen thousand feet of it—enough for a three-hour show. Now we had the picture in the can but didn't know what to do with the can. We had a private showing for the actors and members of the staff. I waited expectantly for glowing praise.

When the lights went up, the entire company was seen quickly sneaking out, and their manner plainly indicated what they thought of it. Some did stop to remark, "Oh! it was fine. We enjoyed it so much," etc., but I wasn't fooled. Afterwards I overheard this frank comment among themselves, "What a shame. Mr. Griffith spent all that money and time—such poor results."

So I tried it out before a regular audience in the theatre—also in New York with the staff and other friends. The problem now was how we could exhibit the picture and at least get our money back. The film was too long for the regular moving picture theatre, so the staff proposed we show it for ten, twenty, and thirty-five cents in some regular theatre and here I shall have to pay an apology, a quarter-century overdue, to Mr. George M. Cohan, that great good fellow and superb actor, who is still going strong.

In 1915 there were only two shows in New York doing any real business. One of these was a Cohan show. Even a producer like Mr. Cohan will get a production now and then that lays an egg. After seeing one of these shows, I proclaimed to the staff that if they would pay $2.50 (that being the top price in that period) to see this show, they certainly would pay two dollars to see *The Birth of a Nation*.

Some of the staff seemed to think we might try this experiment, but here again Mr. Dixon got busy. He sent all of us—individually and collectively—long letters dripping with sarcasm and telegrams of burning indignation against such an "absurd" idea. The gist was "Ask people to pay $2 to see a moving picture! Well, keep out of the park, or the squirrels will certainly get you."

Finally, we rented a theatre and tried to put the show in on percentage so we would not have to put up any cash, but the New York managers were too smart for that. They figured a percentage would net them small potatoes, so they let us have the theatre very cheap. Then the opposition opened fire. Various carpetbagger associations, plus the *New York World*—morning and evening editions—put up a squawk, and the license bureau refused to give the theatre a license.

We spent hectic hours and days—yes, weeks—with our lawyers, headed by the famous Martin W. Littleton, before various committees, the license bureau, and finally the mayor. Incidentally, this happened in all the large cities in the North. It kept us on the sleepless jump for a long time, but finally the mayor of New York City broke the ice and allowed it to be shown.

The opposition was there in full force at the premiere. A riot was brewing. Over the boos, catcalls, and hisses were the whistles and applause. It became a contest. The booers tried to drown out the applauders and vice versa. We were frightened out of our wits for fear of a riot—for that would have been the end of *The Birth of a Nation*.

Some of those who opposed the showing of the picture had thoughtfully brought a lot of very old eggs. One fellow, a poor shot, in-

95

stead of hitting the screen, plumped a couple of the worst possible eggs right on the "bean" of a bald-headed Dutchman who played the bass violin. His loud and indignant protests were lost in the general tumult. He dared not cease playing. He seemed to think the whole orchestra would collapse if he stopped sawing. So there he was, smelly eggs cascading down his bald head over his face, trying vainly to shake off the substance, but his devotion to his art would not allow him to stop playing for even one minute. Finally the picture came to a close. The eggs and vegetables were gathered up by the janitor, and we went out to sit up all night and wait for the morning papers.

The first paper that we read that dawn gave us the old stingeree. It was the *New York World*. Perhaps they were evening their score with me for slipping them that fake cookery story years ago. Anyhow, they applied the paddle where it hurt most. We were in despair. A prickly, goosefleshy feeling ascended from my ankles to the top of my scalp. I dared not look down because I was sure the "old varmint" was rubbing right against my ankles. But when the other papers came out, some of their reviews, particularly that of the *Tribune* and Dorothy Dix, made the Thackerays, Fieldings, Dickenses, and other authors fade into the background, at least as far as I was concerned.

The next afternoon I went around to see how the box office was getting on. There was a serpentine line about a block long trying to buy tickets. Of course, besides good notices, the picture had found an especially good front-page press by virtue of its being banned.

After the matinee I returned to the Astor Hotel, and Mike, the old doorkeeper, said, "You know, it's a peculiar thing, Mr. Griffith. I'm sure I didn't take enough drinks last night to cause me to be seeing things, but I swear I just saw something that looked like a wolf running lickety-split away from you. He jumped right over my head, broke two windows and took a short cut through the hotel lobby."

Alas, later I got a brain storm and made *Intolerance*. Unlike *The Birth of a Nation*, this cost me a barrel of dough. A few days after the opening of *Intolerance* in New York, I went into the theatre to see how the business was. After wandering around in the dark, barking my ankles on the empty chairs, looking vainly for the audience, I discovered that to all practical purposes, the only occupant of the theatre was my old furry shadow.

The Birth of a Nation, however, might be said to have caused the shotgun wedding of the stage and the movies.

something that looked like a wolf running lickety-split
away from you. He jumped right over my head, broke two
windows and took a short cut through the hotel lobby.

Alas, later I got a brain-storm and made
"Intolerance". Unlike the "Birth of A Nation", this cost
me a barrel of dough. A few days after the opening of
"Intolerance" in New York, I went into the theatre to see
how the business was. After wandering around in the dark,
barking my ankles on the empty chairs, looking vainly for
the audience, I discovered that to all practical purposes,
the only occupant of the theatre was my old furry shadow.

*The "Birth of a Nation", however, might be said to have
caused the shotgun wedding of the stage and the movies.*

D. W. Griffith

O.K.

Henry B. Walthall and
Blanche Sweet;
Judith of Bethulia,
1914.

The first American four-reeler; Lillian Gish; *Judith of Bethulia*, 1914.

Blanche Sweet and Kate Bruce, one of Griffith's favorite character actresses; *Judith of Bethulia*, 1914.

Judith was the last movie Griffith made for Biograph; Blanche Sweet; *Judith of Bethulia*, 1914.

Lillian Gish and Blanche Sweet; *Judith of Bethulia*, 1914.

An ad for
The Birth of a Nation,
1915.

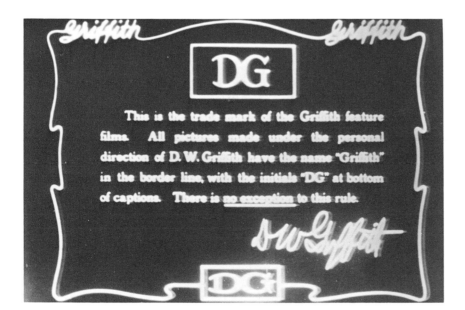

To protect his films (and,
no doubt, to give credit
where it was due),
Griffith ran this imprimatur
on *The Birth of a Nation,* 1915.

The principals in the film: Henry Walthall as the Little Colonel and
Lillian Gish as Elsie Stoneman; *The Birth of a Nation*, 1915.

Mae Marsh as Flora Cameron,
the Little Colonel's sister;
The Birth of a Nation, 1915.

Miriam Cooper as Margaret Cameron;
The Birth of a Nation, 1915.

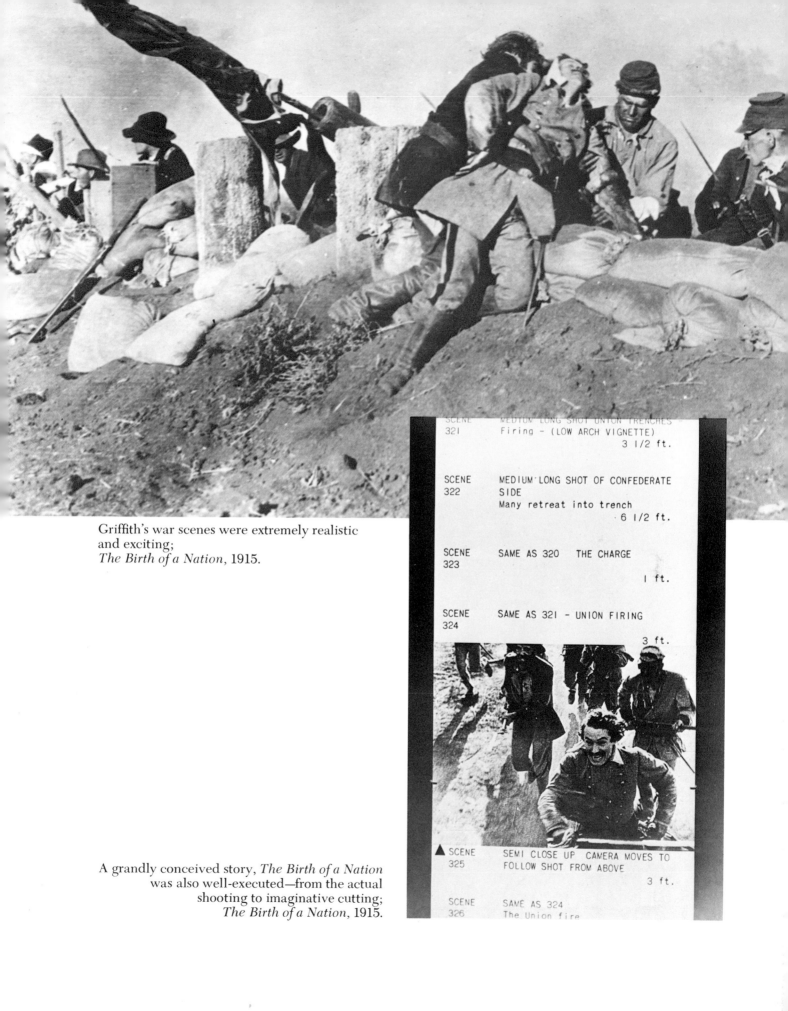

Griffith's war scenes were extremely realistic and exciting;
The Birth of a Nation, 1915.

SCENE 321   MEDIUM LONG SHOT UNION TRENCHES – Firing – (LOW ARCH VIGNETTE)
                   3 1/2 ft.

SCENE 322   MEDIUM LONG SHOT OF CONFEDERATE SIDE
Many retreat into trench
                   6 1/2 ft.

SCENE 323   SAME AS 320   THE CHARGE
                   1 ft.

SCENE 324   SAME AS 321 – UNION FIRING
                   3 ft.

SCENE 325   SEMI CLOSE UP   CAMERA MOVES TO FOLLOW SHOT FROM ABOVE
                   3 ft.

SCENE 326   SAME AS 324
The Union fire

A grandly conceived story, *The Birth of a Nation* was also well-executed—from the actual shooting to imaginative cutting;
The Birth of a Nation, 1915.

Griffith used almost every directorial technique devised in this one masterful film. This scene was strengthened by the iris effect; *The Birth of a Nation*, 1915.

"War's Peace" was a cruel climax; *The Birth of a Nation*, 1915.

Howard Gaye as General Lee and Donald Crisp, extreme right, as General Grant;
The Birth of a Nation, 1915.

Raoul Walsh as John Wilkes Booth
and Joseph Henabery as Abraham Lincoln;
The Birth of a Nation, 1915.

The controversial part of the film
was Griffith's portrayal of Reconstruction
and the Negro role in it;
The Birth of a Nation, 1915.

Walter Long (made up with burnt cork)
as Gus, the renegade Negro,
with clansmen (including John Ford);
The Birth of a Nation, 1915.

Billy Bitzer and D. W. Griffith.
Bitzer worked as Griffith's cameraman
from the Biograph days through
the early 1920s.

Wall posters to advertise *The Birth of a Nation*; the film cost $100,000 to make
and grossed more than $18 million over the years.

. . . and Some Notes

EDITOR'S NOTE: At this point, my collaboration on D. W. Griffith's autobiography ceased, due to his hasty return to Hollywood. The manuscript was a first draft, loosely written, and contained errors that Griffith might have rectified had the collaboration continued.

Fortunately, we had sketched out the complete book before the actual writing began, and due to Griffith's insistence upon "rehearsals," these rambling notes covered his entire career from his birth on a farm near Centerfield, Kentucky, to the making of his last picture. Except for basic material needed for continuity, information from the Griffith papers that is known to have been frequently published was deleted.

President Wilson said that *The Birth of a Nation* was like "writing history with lightning," and Lenin, immediately alert to the propoganda uses of the motion picture, called it "an express train among pushcarts."

When Mitchell's batteries of press agents and McCarthy's dozen road companies had done their work, the United States was refighting the Civil War while Europe was embroiled in the World War I, and D. W. Griffith's little band of actors and actresses was famous in every capital. The publicity campaign was carried on Harry Aitken's books as a $47,000 liability—but the name of the man from Centerfield was up in lights around the world. Hollywood's directors were quick to grasp that here, within the confines of a single motion picture, were all the basic techniques needed for a complete medium of expression.

The picture is supposed to have grossed no less than $18 million, and D. W. Griffith became a millionaire twice over and tax free. Thomas Dixon, the author, was reported to have been paid a million dollars for a story from which only three pages were used. Mutual Pictures' Board of Directors collected a half-million dollars for their initial investment of $25,000. William Clune, the Los Angeles theater man, received $300,000 for his timely $15,000 stake; and John Barry, the secretary to whom Mr. Griffith had given a $700 commission, received $15,000 for plowing that fee back into the picture.

Like Louis B. Mayer, whose showing of *The Birth of a Nation* in Massachusetts earned him $400,000, many an exhibitor earned enough money from this one picture to turn movie producer himself. Some retired wealthy. Due to a loose system of accounting, there were others of whom Griffith said, "Possibly they were not dishonest, but we could have made a hell of a lot more money without them." For this reason, no one knows to this day how much the picture actually grossed. Estimates have run as high as $48 million. And at the time, the picture was shown in only eleven states.

The Birth of a Nation was sold out for forty-seven weeks at the Liberty Theater in New York and earned a half-million dollars in that house alone, a performance which was duplicated by the Majestic Theater in Brooklyn. The picture ran a year in Boston and Chicago and fifteen years in the South. Nine years before the opening of *The Birth of a Nation* at the Liberty Theater, Dixon's *The Clansman,* with Griffith playing one of the leads, had failed miserably as a stage play.

It was argued that the war in Europe had conditioned customers for *The Birth of a Nation*'s panoramic battle scenes. America, however, had forgotten what war was really like, and the sequences of soldiers waving flags while they died on ramparts found a ready audience in 1915.

D. W. Griffith's excesses of sentimentality in this great picture were smothered by his brilliant camera techniques, but his handling of the postwar slaves led to a charge of racism. Contrary to editorials of that day, however, D. W. Griffith's story was not an indictment of the Negro race as portrayed in the original Dixon story, but neither was it fair-minded. "Within the facts," said Albert Bigelow Paine, "but hardly within the proprieties."

Despite the claims advanced in later years, some by D. W. Griffith himself, *The Birth of a Nation* was not the first movie to tour the country as a road show, *Quo Vadis?* and D'Annunzio's weak *Cabiria* having been handled in this manner. Nor did it possess the first musical score to attend a motion picture as some have claimed. Saint-Saens wrote music for a French picture in 1908. There were other claims equally as meretricious, but due to the techniques, *The Birth of a Nation* would have been a great picture had the story been concerned with *The Adventures of Dollie,* Griffith's first picture.

Any evaluation of genius rests inevitably

on dangerous ground, but in the case of David Wark Griffith, certain facts appear self-evident. First a shy, sensitive country boy with a jerry-built education and then a knockabout stage actor, he possessed at no time the background or mental equipment to evaluate flattery. After *The Birth of a Nation* flickered around the world, the adulation of the millions and the outraged cries of racism from press and pulpit blew him from one shore to another, finally shoaling him into a lonely lighthouse not entirely of his own making. In 1915, in this hour of triumph, the ministry and press thundered that D. W. Griffith had committed a sinful act. And Centerfield had heard. At one time a petition was actually raised in the East to outlaw the motion picture industry, and now D. W. Griffith desperately sought to win over his detractors with advertisements and interviews that bordered upon the maudlin.

In all this turmoil and fanfare, Griffith had little time to savor his great achievement. He told me that the night after the riotous Liberty Theater opening, he hailed a hansom cab and toured the Bowery, revisiting the scenes of his youthful despair. Then he satisfied an overweening ambition: he dined alone in the window of Luchow's Restaurant on Fourteenth Street, "just like Mansfield and Belasco and Shaw." (This hour probably marked the only point in his career that he was not beset by problems of financial survival.) Then he went back to his hotel, put in a call to Centerfield, and fell asleep.

In the streets below Griffith's hotel that night, crowds mobbed the newsboys. The Germans had sunk the *Lusitania.*

With the passing of the great liner, the barnacled fashion of Queen Victoria's days was finally laid to rest, but D. W. Griffith was already busy with the idea of a "silent symphony"—a new motion picture that would surpass even *The Birth of a Nation.*

The Silent Symphony
Intolerance

The Birth of a Nation whetted the appetite of almost everyone in the motion picture industry. After making a contract quickie on the coast, D. W. Griffith returned to New York, tired and discouraged. He wanted a free rein and no more "sausages." Harry Aitken, his producer at Mutual, told Griffith that he, Aitken, was withdrawing from Mutual Pictures and that Ad Kessel, the discoverer of Charlie Chaplin, and his partner, Charlie Bauman, were deserting the New York Motion Picture Company, taking along all their directors, actors, and actresses. It was their answer to Adolph Zukor and his glittering Famous Players.

Aitken pointed out that Griffith would be working again with his old friend, Mack Sennett, but Griffith pointed out that Tom Ince also worked for Kessel. (Ince and Griffith were incompatible.) Aitken promised Griffith the free rein he wanted, however, and the director acquiesced.

As plans for the coup went forward, D. W. Griffith proceeded with Mutual's picture schedule. By this time, he had inaugurated an informal school for directors and would wave his old straw hat (his "lucky" one from *The Birth of a Nation*) and happily expound on his theories of picture-making to his novice directors until the entire company would be standing by. And from those impromptu sessions under the California pepper trees were graduated such directors as Frank Lloyd, Victor Fleming, Eric von Stroheim, Donald Crisp, John Emerson, W. Christy Cabanne, Raoul Walsh, W. S. Van Dyke, and Elmer Clifton, to mention a few, including a young clan rider from *The Birth of a Nation* named John Ford.

The attacks upon the narrow social significance of *The Birth of a Nation* had set D. W. Griffith to mounting a counteroffensive. The startling fact that people would actually throw things and hit each other all because of a shadow play on the screen had impressed him deeply, reminding him of the Flexners' discussions of the brawling Greek plays wherein the customer brought his lunch, screamed his opinions, stayed all day, and got his money's worth. Only a real medium of art could arouse a people to such an action.

D. W. Griffith needed another controversial topic when he made a picture called *The Mother and the Law* with Bobby Harron and Mae Marsh. He had finally grasped his theme. Slowly a broad story began to rise and take shape in his mind—a towering story of the absurdities of prejudice down through the ages. He began reading Zola.

The incubus of *Intolerance* had begun to rise in Griffith's mind in 1912. That year *Quo Vadis?*, an Italian picture based on Nero's Coliseum trials of the Christians, was booked into the old Astor Theater in New York and packed them in for weeks. Griffith

111

himself never admitted to witnessing *Quo Vadis?*, but it is known that he began reading the Bible in his hotel room at that time for something other than spiritual assistance.

In the fall of 1912 Griffith entrained his little company for Chatsworth, California, a small town some miles from Hollywood, and set up shop. Inspired by a Biblical story written by Thomas Aldrich Bailey, he had a mental script of sorts that he called *Judith of Bethulia*. The Front Office had given him a budget of $18,000.

For weeks Griffith rehearsed his players on a guarded lot. They would toss off a "sausage" and go back to work on *Judith*. Costs rose to $36,000, and Biograph hired a certified public accountant. If *Judith* had been released promptly, Griffith probably could have saved face—and his job. Biograph, however, shelved *Judith* for a year, then released it at the same rate as a quickie: ten cents a foot. It was a box office loser at that price, and Griffith was called before the Board of Directors, given the empty title of supervisor, and forbidden to direct any more pictures for Biograph. *Judith of Bethulia*, however, like *The Mother and the Law* and Linda Arvidson's *Charity*, was an early litmus of the *Intolerance* mystique that was already rising in his mind.

Then one hot summer night in 1915, D. W. Griffith met secretly with Aitken, Kessel, Bauman, Ince, and Sennett in La Junta, Colorado, and the Triangle Film Corporation was born. Each producer had his own star director. Ince's unit would be known as Fine Arts Pictures; Sennett's as Keystone Komedies; Griffith's as Master Pictures.

Harry Aitken coined The Master tag during his last days with Mutual, reflecting his lucrative $25,000 investment in *The Birth of a Nation*. Now he ballyhooed his corner of Triangle and even encouraged lesser employees to refer to D. W. Griffith as The Master. Thus did this busy man and his flacks nurture the mystique of D. W. Griffith. Crassness and absurdity were the order of the day in Hollywood, and the man from Centerfield now began to believe his own publicity. The new mahatma gathered converts, and although he had encountered small opportunity to listen to arty twaddle about his ideas before this, he now sprinkled his conversation with such large terms as "individuality in creative free enterprise production" and "kinetic energy of aesthetics in amoral scansions of empirical doubt." Later, the successors to these literary ecdysiasts wrote pieces about the avant-garde genius of D. W. Griffith for experimental cinema periodicals—essays that always seemed to be on the point of profundities, but never quite gelled. Although Triangle was already saturating the market with publicity on Griffith, Ince, and Sennett, the man from Centerfield felt that he wasn't getting his share and now formed the D. W. Griffith Service, his personal publicity organization, with his brother and manager, Albert Grey, as editor and publisher. (Griffith said his brother adopted the name Grey "to avoid confusion.") Grey hired flacks to insure that Griffith got his due as *the* artist in residence at Triangle, and the initial press releases were signed by Griffith himself. And so D. W. Griffith, the man who invented Hollywood, became the man whom Hollywood invented. A carefully manufactured legend of The Master, with the benediction of Triangle, began to seep out of Hollywood. It was all sweet music, however, to the man who had been charged with the resurrection of the Ku Klux Klan. Later Griffith, like Picasso, referred to this experience as his Blue Period.

At that time Triangle's roster included Weber and Fields, Eddie Foy, Raymond Hitchcock, De Wolf Hopper, Billie Burke, Willie Collier, Sir Herbert Beerbohm Tree, and William S. Hart. All were established stage stars except Hart, but it was Hart, the second-rate bit player, from whom Triangle profited most.

With a blare of fanfare that boggled even Hollywood, the new company huffed into 4500 Sunset Boulevard, and the Triangle cameras began rolling. The central theme was to make big pictures and charge accordingly. The formation of Triangle Films marked the first time that the movie industry and Wall Street had formally joined hands. Triangle stock now was listed on the curb and the day of private investment was about over.

Ad Kessel hired Douglas Fairbanks in New York and wired Griffith that he was sending the actor on to him because he had guaranteed Fairbanks that D. W. Griffith would make a Master Picture with him. Griffith was not endeared with the acrobatics of the young Broadway stage star, however, and when Fairbanks arrived, Griffith introduced him to Mack Sennett as the latter's new comedy star. Fairbanks balked, and Griffith finally turned him over to an assistant director, Johnny Emerson, and lent the pair Anita Loos to write their screen captions. When the trio became popular, Griffith said brusquely, "They appeal to a class of people I don't make pictures for."

Even as The Master, it wasn't long before D. W. Griffith found himself stereotyped under the same conditions as existed in the old Edison studio. System had become the watchword at Triangle. The efficient Ince now had Aitken's ear, and the budget ruled the set. Being a man who always took off his hat last when undressing for bed, Griffith chafed under the yoke of charts and rows of neat figures. His contract guaranteed him two independent pictures annually, however, and he began to feel more and more that his reputation depended largely upon these free-lance efforts.

Always a loner, D. W. Griffith continued to spend his evenings poring over stacks of books that dealt with greed and intolerance and vested interests. He read of Christ and Napoleon and Lao-tse and the fall of Babylon and the massacre of the Huguenots on St. Bartholomew's Eve. He turned to the newspapers and read of the Stielow case, wherein a young mother's infant had been taken from her forcibly by reformers; of nineteen men being shot and bludgeoned to death by police and company guards in a chemical plant strike.

In his hotel room Griffith chiseled out four parallel stories of history, exposing the easy virtue of public opinion. Babylon. Jerusalem. Paris. New York. He followed the betrayal of Babylon to the Persians; the perfidy of Judas and the cries of the mob behind Pilate; the suppression of religious freedom in France and the hysterical slaughter of the Huguenots; and lastly, he contrived a modern story of treachery and love in the slums of New York. Now he could see these stories flowing together, until they approached a confluence of meaning for the brotherhood of man.

Griffith said that John Carl Briel, a Los Angeles composer, had taught him about a musical fugue when they were discussing the score for *The Birth of a Nation.* (The director himself was unschooled in music.)

Some sort of symbol, an amalgam, was needed to tie this dramatic fugue together. He found his literary catalyst one night in Walt Whitman's *Leaves of Grass:*

". . . endlessly rocks the cradle,
   Uniter of here and hereafter."

He pictured a woman rocking the cradle of humanity, a symbol of hope and life eternal.

A hundred titles were discarded before the director finally decided upon *Intolerance.* The story itself, like *The Birth of a*

113

Nation, was etched on his mind. Again, he needed no script.

When Griffith sketched out his big picture idea to the front office, he encountered no difficulty with investment capital, and first-rank Hollywood folk fought to buy a piece of his second independent picture. (*The Birth of a Nation* was still making more money than some of Triangle's latest releases.)

Intolerance was swiftly financed, and D. W. Griffith started to work. Weeks were consumed in planning sets and hiring a cast. Griffith engaged assistant directors, cameramen, and technicians by the dozen—and extras by the thousand. Costumes were ordered in box-car lots. A small army of carpenters began hammering and sawing on the Sunset Boulevard lot. Long rehearsals were scheduled until this company, too, was scene perfect and imbued with the spirit of the picture.

By this time Griffith's backers had begun to tug at his sleeves, but he faced them down.

Crowds of sidewalk superintendents began to gather on Sunset Boulevard to goggle as the walls of the huge Babylonian set went up—three hundred feet, and stretching out almost a half-mile long.

The entire Griffith lot was bedlam except to the man in the straw hat atop a wooden tower. The great director was using four different casts, one for each of his stories. While the camera ground away, assistant directors yelled themselves hoarse, the mob of actors roiled around in a quartet of historical periods, and the man from Centerfield waved his arms from atop the tower in a preset code of signals: a puppeteer directing an organized riot.

Griffith had four movements in counterpoint in this "symphony," hoping that each movement would complement the other and produce a cumulative effect. Movement itself was the shock value of his com-

position. In sequence development, he planned to gain dynamic suspense by intercutting scenes for accent and flashing back for clarity. And through it all, he iris-dissolved a woman rocking a cradle. This was his symphony. He forgot about dissonance.

Costs mounted, and when the bills reached $12,000 a day, Griffith's backers called a conference. One baiting remark led to another and ended with D. W. Griffith giving each backer a note for the amount he had invested in the picture.

Everything D. W. Griffith owned was now staked on *Intolerance.*

The Big Picture rolled on. Anyone in Hollywood not in the cast of *Intolerance* held gossip parties for those who were. (Two decades later, *Gone with the Wind* duplicated this first social tidal wave in the movie colony.)

The colony tingled when the Persian horde attacked Babylon under an artificial sky for an effect of depth and impending doom. This device became known as "the process shot."

They watched as the man with the hooked nose and flinting eyes now innovated the "trucking camera" to follow his mob scenes and even panned the Babylonian set from a balloon. During the trial in the modern story in *Intolerance,* Griffith sought an effect of anguish from the young mother sitting on the witness stand. He wanted the viewer to experience her emotions. So he had Billy Bitzer shoot only the tightly clasped hands of the young woman. In such manner did D. W. Griffith give life to the screen. These efforts at subtle interpretation were later lifted by von Stroheim and many others and used until threadbare and bromidic. Griffith continued to devise techniques as the need arose, and not a few embryonic directors—then bit players or extras—watched their development and mentally stored them away for future use. Many times David

Wark Griffith was to see himself repeated on the screen under some strange aliases.

As *Intolerance* swept on, only the man on the tower could maintain any clear conception of the madness below. He alone held the dramatic values as he twiddled and jerked his marionette strings and coaxed the picture along.

Through the entire epic plot of *Intolerance*, however, ran a curious skein: a sadistic warp and a sentimental woof. Never before had so much violence been shown on the screen; yet we find the heroine titled Dear One and the hero listed as The Boy. Repressed by Victorian taboos on sex, he found an outlet in brutality and gore.

As his classic drew to a close, the director's fever mounted proportionately, and he drove his people night and day. Four broad sequences were now being shot: Christ was shown stumbling up Calvary; Belshazzar and Babylon were feasting while the Persians attacked the city's gates; the Huguenots were being massacred in France; and in New York an automobile carrying a young mother clutching a governor's pardon sped to the prison where her husband already stood on the gallows.

When the picture was done, Griffith's assistants handed him the shining cans of film, and *Intolerance* was his alone.

With Jimmy and Rose Smith, his longtime film cutters, D. W. Griffith tackled the raw *Intolerance.* For many days and nights they whacked away at fifty-seven miles of film. Many were the faces left on the cutting room floor when Griffith and his young assistants completed their task. Much of the artistic triumph claimed for *Intolerance* in later years was due to the boldness and skill of Jimmy and Rose Smith (and, of course, to the wizardry of cameraman Billy Bitzer).

When Griffith and his two helpers finally laid aside the shears, they found that the cast in the finished picture included Lillian Gish, Bobby Harron, Mae Marsh, Carmel Myers, Bessie Love, Tully Marshal, Mildred Harris Chaplin, Douglas Fairbanks, Elmo Lincoln, Carol Dempster, De Wolf Hopper, Constance Talmadge, Alma Rubens, Sir Herbert Tree, Alfred Paget, Seena Owen, Monte Blue, Gloria Swanson, Eric von Stroheim, and George Fawcett. Some of these people were established stage stars; others, like Eric von Stroheim and Gloria Swanson, were unknown.

It is curious that Linda Arvidson, Griffith's first wife, whom he claimed he never saw again after their separation in 1911, now produced a picture called *Charity* with Frank Powell, an old Biograph actor. *Charity* purported to be an exposé of the orphanage racket in New York City. Mrs. D. W. Griffith wrote the scenario. It was probably more than coincidence that Mae Marsh was being pictured at the same time in *Intolerance* as a victim of a corrupt orphan asylum, but when Griffith was later asked about this parallel script, the director only pulled his nose and said, "Well, that's all past now, but *Charity* proved a good stalking horse for *Intolerance,* didn't it?"

Several religious organizations had pilloried Mrs. Griffith's picture until it was withdrawn. It seems that Griffith was actively seeking the same type of publicity evoked by *The Birth of a Nation.*

Intolerance opened at the Liberty Theater September 6, 1916. Sentiment and superstition had caused D. W. Griffith to book his second big picture into the scene of his first major triumph over the motion picture industry. He also registered at the same hotel where he had slept, fully dressed, after the memorable opening of *The Birth of a Nation.* He was careful to put on his shoes in the same sequence in which he had taken them off.

There was a full house that night at the old Liberty when *Intolerance* opened. Long queues, brought by the success of *The Birth of a Nation,* still stood outside the box office

115

when the Standing Room Only sign went up. When the story flashed on the screen there was a polite ripple of applause for the early scenes. Then, as the four stories intertwined, there was silence. Nobody yelled, and nobody threw anything.

The director stayed up and waited for the morning paper. The kindest critic said, "*Intolerance* is a lesson in calculus to a public that only yesterday learned the multiplication tables."

The afternoon papers added the *coup de grâce*. One reviewer dismissed *Intolerance* as being in the same status "as a joke that has to be explained."

Intolerance was purely an artist's response to society. The director wanted the moviegoer to find an experience—an experience leading outward to a larger world. It is said that every valid piece of art represents the response of the artist to his total experience as a living man. In this light, the man from Centerfield became identified with Genghis Khan's captured rug weaver who wove beautiful stories in an unknown tongue.

The critics of that day included such distinguished thinkers as Burns Mantle, Percy Hammond, George Jean Nathan, Heywood Broun, and Alexander Woollcott. But they, too, were guilty of making easy generalizations about *Intolerance*.

Twenty years later when *Intolerance* was released for exhibition to a number of universities, one New York critic wrote, "It is not flattering to the current screen to report that in March, 1936, the most interesting and provocative picture of the month was D. W. Griffith's *Intolerance* . . . ."

Oddly enough, the Russians seemed to be the only people who liked what they saw in *Intolerance* in 1916. One print of the picture was stolen from a Berlin vault and doctored by the Russians to the extent that Griffith seemed to be an apostle of Lenin.

For all that, the American public might have reacted somewhat differently had the picture been distributed six months sooner. Early in 1916, D. W. Griffith had been caught with a pacifist motion picture just as the United States prepared to go to war.

As the U.S. moved closer to war, the government stepped into the censorship scrap over *Intolerance* and lent the services of its own propaganda agencies to the various so-called patriotic organizations. In a few weeks *Intolerance* was nationally condemned. In many cities the picture was barred altogether.

Later in his career, after his meeting with President Harding, a number of high government officials confided to D. W. Griffith that Washington, conscious of the mass hysteria provoked by *The Birth of a Nation*, had feared *Intolerance* might well have sparked an explosion of antiwar feeling throughout the U.S. just as President Wilson had decided that war was inevitable. So the government shot what was left of *Intolerance* in the back of the head.

Ad for *Intolerance*
. . . A Sun Play of the Ages;
1916.

Rev. A. W. McClure
as Father Farley comforts
Bobby Harron in the modern
story; *Intolerance*, 1916.

Mae Marsh in the modern story; *Intolerance*, 1916.

The gigantic set for the Babylon sequence; *Intolerance*, 1916.

Constance Talmadge
and Alfred Paget;
Intolerance, 1916.

Alfred Paget as
Belshazzar and
Seena Owen as the
Princess Beloved;
Intolerance, 1916.

Grandly conceived and monumentally executed, including wild chariot rides; *Intolerance*, 1916.

Costuming was opulent
in the medieval French story;
Intolerance, 1916.

Josephine Crowell as Catherine de Medici surveys the result of the St. Bartholomew's Massacre;
Intolerance, 1916.

From Broken Blossoms *to* Way Down East

Intolerance had cost D. W. Griffith nearly $2 million—his profits from *The Birth of a Nation.* Shelving his pride, he went to work for Adolph Zukor and the latter's Artcraft Pictures, along with Sennett and Ince. Zukor had virtually bought out Triangle and had raided the Broadway stage, too. This was the situation, shortly after the United States declared war on Germany April 6, 1917, when Charles S. Hart, a Hearst executive and director of the government's film propaganda division, sought out D. W. Griffith to head the President's first Liberty Loan drive.

So D. W. Griffith put aside his differences with the government and toured the nation with Mary Pickford and Charlie Chaplin, and, sometimes, Douglas Fairbanks. (Later Griffith confided that "Fairbanks wasn't invited but came along anyway.")

During one such loan tour, Griffith received a telegram from Washington, D.C. He was invited to the White House.

In Washington, President Wilson and the film director exchanged pleasantries briefly in the former's study on the second floor. (When asked in 1939 what he remembered best about this conversation, he responded quickly, "I was thinking about all the leading hotels and private clubs where motion picture people had been barred.")

Never one for small talk, Wilson came to the point. "Since you've filmed so many make-believe wars, Mr. Griffith, my as-sociates have led me to believe that you might like to go to England and possibly tour the battlefields of France and make some pictures showing our fight for democracy."

Within a few minutes, Griffith forgot all about the government's scuttling of *Intolerance.* The President stressed that this would be "a war to end all wars," and soon Griffith, the erstwhile pacifist, was believing it, too. Griffith went to England first, then sent for his featured players from the old Triangle company, including the Gish sisters, Bobby Harron, Henry Walthall, and Eric von Stroheim.

Upon his arrival in Southampton, a ship news reporter gave Griffith a bad moment over a garbled quote from Dickens, but once ashore he was quick to buy a collector's set of Dickens from a bookstall and also a copy of Thomas Burke's *Limehouse Nights.* He was delighted to learn that *The Birth of a Nation* had just completed a long run at the Drury Lane Theater in London and that *Intolerance* had just opened at the same theater. Zepplins were bombing the Drury Lane area nightly, but still the crowds came. England was losing a million men in France, but she could still applaud a pacifist picture.

The great director was immediately taken in tow by such social figures as Lord Beaverbrook and Lord Cholmondeley, and he now began to dress as, Alexander Woollcott said, "as if someone were about to strike a highly polished brass gong." When he discovered a plurality of worn and faded tweeds one day among the peers visiting the Griffith lot, however, he promptly repaired to a secondhand clothes stall and appeared on location the next day in worn and faded tweed, too. While Griffith insisted upon his company's living in cloistered quarters and frowned upon any extracurricular activities, he himself was busy lunching with David Lloyd George, the Prime Minister, fox-hunting with Lord Beaverbrook, and attending Red Cross teas and charity bazaars in his honor.

The director's trip through France was sponsored by the British and French governments, and he had been promised a look at troops in action.

Griffith found a bombed-out French village for the locale of *Hearts of the World,* a tale of a French hamlet in occupied territory subjected to Prussian brutality. British and French forces were preparing for the drive on the Aisne as Griffith prepared to shoot his picture. He learned that men did not die in a modern war charging ramparts with flying banners. The sight of real war sickened him and he said later that he regretted his part in it, recalling how agitated he had become when preaching against war in *The Birth of a Nation* and *Intolerance.*

Back in England, Griffith quickly finished *Hearts of the World* on interior sets and Lord Beaverbrook's Leatherwood estate. While completing this picture he received a phone call from George Bernard Shaw. Would Mr. Griffith have lunch with him?

Over his milk and crackers at Claridge's, Shaw tried to sell the director a thick manuscript for the movies. Griffith said later that he never learned the title of the story because they got into an argument (he couldn't remember about what), ending with Shaw's rising and giving a lecture to the entire dining room on what was wrong with Hollywood and the motion picture business. Griffith left abruptly, and the irascible Irishman never forgot or forgave D. W. Griffith and for years sniped at him through the press.

Griffith's next picture, *The Great Love,* was shot on Lady Mary Paget's estate near London. At the time, it was said to have been almost too faulty to be released, partly because Griffith had fallen in love with an English bit player, Lady Diana Manners. The renowned beauty introduced the maker of *Intolerance* to the Astor set, who promptly lionized him until the director forgot why he had come to England. Many years later, Lady Manners wrote that she could never quite bring herself to tell this "oddly reserved American" that she wanted "very much to tour America as an actress." But D. W. Griffith—with a blank movie contract in his pocket—had been frozen to silence by an awesome pedigree.

Late in life, Griffith confessed that he had forgotten many details of that period but not Lady Manners, "daughter of a hundred earls, whose shimmering beauty" was still retained in the retina of his eye "like the smile of the Cheshire Cat in *Alice in Wonderland* after the cat itself had vanished." He added that he never told Lady Manners of his true feeling for her.

His schedule completed, the director was preparing to return to the States when Lord Beaverbrook informed him that it had been arranged to present Griffith to the Queen Mother.

Two days later, D. W. Griffith marched into Buckingham Palace in top hat, cutaway, and morning trousers. When the great double doors opened, he tried to remember the protocol Lord Beaverbrook had schooled him on, but for the first time in his life forgot a rehearsal. The maker of *Intolerance* was not unaccustomed to regal scenes, but this was the real thing. He recalled that after bowing, he was appallingly mute, but the Queen touched his sleeve and said, "Don't be nervous, Mr. Griffith. Tell me what you think of our motion picture industry." After that, they got on. Later he referred again and again to this incident as his greatest hour.

When the New York reporters boarded Griffith's ship, he found himself a greater celebrity than when he had left. He told them that "real war made poor drama," a quote he was to regret.

Shortly after Griffith's return, Hiram Abrams, one of Zukor's idea men, visited him at the Alexandria Hotel and asked if Griffith remembered Oscar Price. The latter had been a government press agent under William G. McAdoo, Secretary of the Treasury, during the war and had organized junkets of Hollywood folk in connection with the Liberty Loan drives.

"I've been talking with Price," said Abrams, "and he thinks you and Pickford, Fairbanks, and Chaplin were on the right track with that idea about a distributing company of your own." He added that he had already talked to the others, and they liked the idea.

"The middle man will be eliminated," pointed out Abrams, "and we'll all slice the box office melon. As a producing director, you can write your own ticket." The last remark was all Griffith remembered.

While the talks went on, Griffith made several pictures for Artcraft, including *A Romance of Happy Valley*. It was another cheap melodrama about boy makes good in the big city, returns home in time to save his family from the poorhouse. Home, in this case, was D. W. Griffith's boyhood home in Kentucky, and there were several scenes of remarkable rural beauty, including a nineteenth-century revival meeting that had documentary quality.

Abrams eventually formed the producing company, hustled Oscar Price into the job as president, and got McAdoo to act as counsel. Ben Schulberg, another Zukor assistant, was picked as executive producer, with Abrams as general manager. D. W. Griffith was production director. Price talked about forming a theater chain and Schulberg explained to the press that stars and directors had become so expensive that no studio could afford to maintain them on a permanent payroll for only one or two pictures a year. It was a lesson in finance that was lost on Griffith. All he could see was his new flexibility as director.

United Artists was a reality.

A few months later, however, Schulberg formed his own distributing company. The loss of Schulberg was disastrous for Griffith. The little man was a brilliant financier, organizer, and a consummate diplomat, and perhaps the only qualified man in the industry who could wave off Griffith's sycophants and persuade him to listen to reason. (Griffith always had a pensive and thoughtful recollection of Schulberg.)

D. W. Griffith's beginning with United Artists was identical with his start with Mutual Pictures. A quick row of potboilers formed his first schedule. But he was aware of his new freedom now that he was a full-time producer and chafed to get at his first big picture.

While casting about for a story for his first major effort for the new company, he ran across the copy of Burke's *Limehouse Nights* that he had picked up in England. He became fascinated by one of the stories —"The Chink and the Child." It was a tale of a Chinese boy's love for a mistreated white girl. The London setting intrigued him, and he remembered the eeriness of faces swimming out of a Soho fog. In a few weeks he worked out a script of sorts, committed it to memory as usual, and called this screen version *Broken Blossoms*. Actually, he liked the idea of mood created by fog better than he liked the plot.

123

About this time he heard of a cameraman named Hendrik Sardov and plied him with questions. Sardov was a former physics professor and worked with Griffith to produce soft lighting effects. Delighted with his new protégé, Griffith made him assistant to Billy Bitzer, much to that gentleman's dismay.

Griffith noted that the moods of Russian pictures were soundly constructed, but he sensed that they had to be seen like stage plays—from the beginning. (The Russians had gone to school on D. W. Griffith.) These long involved Russian pictures would be rank failures in the United States, he told the press, if shown on a continuous performance basis. The Russian pictures had given him an idea, however, and he now hired an architect and sat up nights sketching plans for a movie theater with an annex. Comedies, short features, and newsreels would be shown in the annex. When the main feature was over, the overflow crowd would be notified on screen, and thus the main theater would fill and empty automatically at the beginning and ending of the feature, "and the picture would be seen as it was intended to be seen."

By the time the architect had finished Griffith's duplex plans, however, the director learned that the nation's theater owners were already building strings of million-dollar palaces without annexes.

More importantly, Griffith had learned something valuable from the Russians—mood development; and from Sardov—soft lighting for such effects. He quickly made two pictures in Florida, then began looking for a studio site away from Hollywood.

As Griffith began work on *Broken Blossoms*, he had the industry in his pocket again. The new picture could make or break United Artists, but the director exuded confidence. Lillian Gish and Richard Barthelmess were cast as the leads. At that time Barthelmess had appeared in only one small picture, but Griffith liked his face. There were only three main characters; and oldtimer Donald Crisp, the heavy, overplayed several major scenes, so busy was he in leading Barthelmess through his first big picture. *Broken Blossoms* was a tragic story with all the leading characters dead at the end, and Griffith was never sure that the public would accept it. There was some stormy dialogue among the United Artists' Big Four as costs rose on the picture, but Griffith bulled his way through the discussions. By now he was a past master at solving myriad contretemps by night while directing a big picture by day.

Griffith said he worked sixteen to eighteen hours a day at that time, particularly on the new dramatic effects. "Mist photography" was employed on the dock scenes and Chinatown vignettes. Love scenes were diffused. Artificial fog was blown onto sets for realism. Griffith perhaps overdid his effects, however, when he devised pastel filters to fit the movie projectors so that pale pink and blue beams could further diffuse the big emotional scenes. Nevertheless, the public, jaded by gray war scenes, hailed such novelties with wild acclaim. A technique more lasting than his newest innovation was his use of close-ups for emphasis and suspense instead of mere conversational intercutting.

Broken Blossoms opened May 13, 1919, in New York at the record price of three dollars for the best seats.

United Artists' first major release was a solid hit, and Richard Barthelmess was suddenly a star of the first magnitude. And for many years thereafter film directors thought of *Broken Blossoms* whenever the subject of mood lighting arose, and of the close-up as the value of what was to be seen rather than the mere enlargement of a face.

On the strength of *Broken Blossoms*, Griffith now released *The Greatest Ques-*

tion, a dismal failure that he had made for another company before the inception of United Artists. Griffith made *The Greatest Question* with the theme of possible communication between the dead and the living. (In England the director had met Sir Arthur Conan Doyle. In America he had spent many hours with Harry Houdini, the famous magician and a Doyle disciple of spiritualism.) It was a flop. Riding the crest of good publicity from *Broken Blossoms,* he stooped to a cheap press agent's trick and was "lost at sea" on a yacht in the Caribbean for six days. It was a front-page story, and *The Greatest Question* was good box office for a short while. He never allowed himself, however, to be hustled into this type of press agentry again.

Behind his new businesslike exterior as a production director, Griffith soon became desperate as he found himself trapped in the current fashion of formula pictures and the beginning of the sex vogue. He found it increasingly difficult to maintain his reputation as an innovator of camera techniques and at the same time familiarize himself with corporate labyrinths. Griffith was learning that being a producer was not an answer to his problems. Somehow, the new flexibility he had enjoyed was dissipating fast. He was losing confidence in himself. Charlie Chaplin had the comedy end of the business; William S. Hart's westerns were all moneymakers; Fairbanks had the costume pictures to himself; and Mary Pickford was earning a million a year. D. W. Griffith saw directors, once his assistants, now making popular pictures and winning fame with his techniques. Then William Fox brought a novelty to the screen—Theda Bara, the first screen siren. And Griffith had to add the sex movie to his growing list of competitors.

By now Hiram Abrams and Oscar Price were feuding over the management control of United Artists. Then Price got embroiled in an argument with Fairbanks and walked out. Price's withdrawal ended United Artists' plans for a theater chain. Block booking had returned as the independent movie houses began drifting back to the big producers to assure a steady flow of pictures. United Artists was in trouble.

Joe Schenck, one of the best organization men in Hollywood, took the helm for a short period, but then Chaplin had an argument with Schenck about the latter's idea to merge United Artists with Metro-Goldwyn-Mayer, and Schenck took a walk.

At this juncture Griffith informed United Artists that he wanted to make a picture about Christ and Napoleon. The story leaked to the press and one trade journal slyly proclaimed: UA TO FILM GRIFFITH STORY.

Then Griffith heard that World Film Corporation, a small producing company, was broke. He remembered that World Film owned a scenario titled *Way Down East,* an old stage melodrama. It was a story of rural New England, and Griffith liked the title. He bought *Way Down East* for $175,000, including $10,000 for Anthony Kelly, the author, to write a screen version. In rapid order, he next bought an old estate with a mansion on a picturesque peninsula at Mamaroneck, Long Island. This was to be his new studio. He said he would never make a picture in Hollywood again.

For the leads in *Way Down East,* Griffith teamed Lillian Gish and Richard Barthelmess again. He also hired John Bunny, the Oliver Hardy of the nickelodeon days, to play Hi Holler, a comic role. (In total eclipse at the time, Bunny gave one of the funniest performances of his career and a classic example of what people laughed at in 1920.)

The plot concerned a country girl seduced by a city slicker. Ordered out into a blizzard by a stern father, she is saved by a neighbor boy, and true love conquers all. It

125

is difficult to believe that Griffith could have got anybody to the box office to witness nineteenth-century soap opera, but again Griffith threw away the script except for a couple pages, as in *The Birth of a Nation,* and began shooting a documentary of rural America that was unsurpassed for its time in authenticity and realism.

The filming of *Way Down East* progressed until the screen idyll needed scenes of great pastoral beauty. Griffith ransacked Long Island for settings that would match memories of his boyhood on the Kentucky farm.

Shooting on *Way Down East* began in the winter. Actually, the first scenes were shot in a blizzard. *Way Down East* entailed some rugged acting. At the confluence of the White River and the Connecticut River, in Vermont, the Griffith company blew out pans of ice with dynamite. Here, Lillian Gish had to ride a cake of ice to the brink of a waterfall before being rescued by Richard Barthelmess. There were no doubles or stunt men. After several retakes, Barthelmess stumbled and fell while running along the bank as Miss Gish, perched on a cake of ice, swirled toward the waterfall. Dangerously close to the brink, Barthelmess managed to sweep her off the ice cake and return to shore. Undaunted, Miss Gish suggested to Griffith that she trail one hand in the icy water for realism. So the scene was reshot.

Again, the picture was structured by Griffith in the cutting room. There were no novelties in *Way Down East* as contrasted with *Broken Blossoms.* The picture received its life and pace simply through his basic shooting techniques, and although at times his cutting skill seemed to have lost cohesion and continuity, it was a soundly made picture.

Way Down East opened in New York and ran for a year, finishing second only to *The Birth of a Nation* in box office gross. Once again D. W. Griffith had made a trashy play into an artistic triumph.

D. W. Griffith meets Alexandria, England's Queen Mother. He described this scene as "my Greatest moment."

Songsheet cover . . . the "authorized popular song response to D. W. Griffith's powerful photodrama. . . ." Bobby Harron and Lillian Gish grace the cover; 1919.

D. W. Griffith and friend. Griffith peremptorily emptied a few bars when accompanied by this pet.

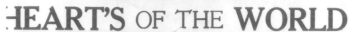

D. W. GRIFFITH'S
WONDER STORY OF THE FILM
HEART'S OF THE WORLD
THE CROWNING TRIUMPH OF A SUPER-GENIUS

SWEETEST
E STORY
R TOLD.

A PARABLE
OF GLORIOUS
FRANCE.

DAVID WARK GRIFFITH

TER **18** MONTHS ON THE BATTLE-FIELDS OF FRANCE.

Respectfully Dedicated to the Super-Genius of the Film—D. W. GRIFFITH

HEARTS OF THE WORLD 5

Words and Music by
Lee-JOHNSON

Published by
Lee-Johnson Music Publishing Co.
LOS ANGELES, CAL.
NEW YORK
LONDON

ALBERT & SON, Sydney, Sole Agents for Australia and New Zealand

This Song is Owned Jointly by Lee Johnson and J. C. Crisler

D W Griffith

LILLIAN GISH

ROBERT HARRON

Lillian Gish and Bobby Harron combine
again on this songsheet cover . . .
"Respectfully Dedicated to the Super-
Genius of the Film—D. W. Griffith."

Ben Alexander and Lillian Gish;
Hearts of the World, 1918.

Griffith was a master at portraying the vicissitudes of old age, war, and poverty; *Hearts of the World*, 1918.

The drama of war as seen through the eyes of a few individuals;
Lillian Gish and Bobby Harron; *Hearts of the World*, 1918.

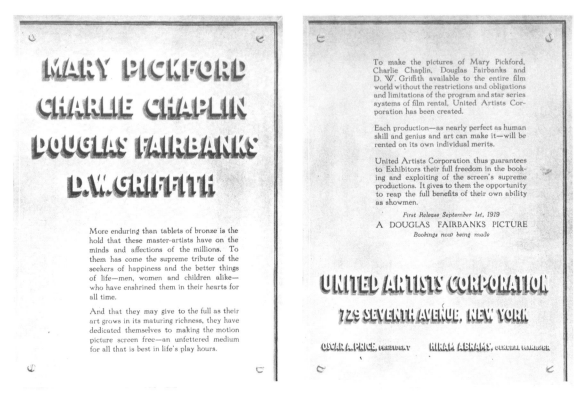

The four United Artists announced their new company with this advertisement in 1919.

An example of Griffith's documentary quality; *Broken Blossoms*, 1919.

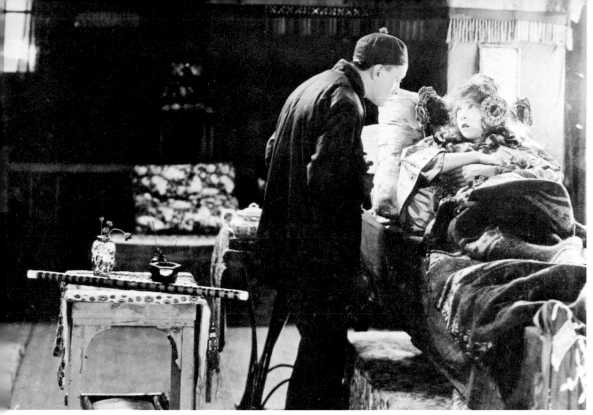

Richard Barthelmess and Lillian Gish; *Broken Blossoms*, 1919.

Richard Barthelmess;
Broken Blossoms, 1919.

Donald Crisp and Lillian Gish;
Broken Blossoms, 1919.

Lillian Gish and Bobby Harron;
True Heart Susie, 1919.

The fast-talking, cigarette-smoking flapper compared unfavorably with Susie,
Griffith's favorite type of heroine; *True Heart Susie*, 1919.

D. W. Griffith
on location for
Way Down East, 1920.

The initial brouhaha was justified as *Way Down East* was a most successful Griffith film.

Lillian Gish; *Way Down East*, 1920.

Lowell Sherman betrays Lillian
Gish; *Way Down East*, 1920.

Richard Barthelmess overcomes
family opposition and an icy
river to rescue Lillian Gish;
Way Down East, 1920.

After re-creating the Civil War and the fall of Babylon, Griffith tackled the French Revolution in *Orphans of the Storm*, 1921.

Lillian Gish, as Henriette, pleads her case to Sidney Herbert as Robespierre; *Orphans of the Storm*, 1921.

Comedienne Dorothy Gish showed her dramatic abilities portraying the blind orphan, Louise. With her is Sheldon Lewis; *Orphans of the Storm*, 1921.

Dorothy (left) and Lillian Gish;
Orphans of the Storm, 1921.

Monte Blue (as Danton) and Lillian Gish;
Orphans of the Storm, 1921.

D. W. Griffith directs the guillotine scene in *Orphans of the Storm*, 1921.

Lucille LaVerne and Dorothy Gish;
Orphans of the Storm, 1921

The orphans,
Lillian and Dorothy Gish;
Orphans of the Storm, 1921.

Pre-Revolution aristocracy considers Griffith's favorite heroine, Lillian Gish; *Orphans of the Storm*, 1921.

Cecil B. DeMille, D. W. Griffith, and Jeanie MacPherson, author of *The King of Kings*. DeMille was one of the many directors who learned their art from The Master.

D. W. Griffith and Mae Marsh on location in the Bayou Teche area of Louisiana; *The White Rose*, 1923.

The Exile of D. W. Griffith

THERE ARE SOME who said that D. W. Griffith's name began to fade after he made *Broken Blossoms;* others said the turning point was *Orphans of the Storm.* The late Kenneth MacGowan, a notable producer and film writer, even contended that Griffith's demise can be traced to *The Birth of a Nation.* Actually, Griffith's decline cannot be measured against any particular picture but rather by what was happening to his audience. Soon after World War I, fashions changed drastically in manners, dress, speech, humor, music, literature, and drama. Americans were becoming sophisticated and Hollywood fell in line with indecent haste.

For anyone born after 1900, the exuberance with which the American people crossed the Victorian frontier is difficult to understand. The war had ended; and now came bathtub gin and the saxophone, the silk step-in and the sex movie. William Fox may have brought the first sex symbol (Theda Bara) to the screen, but Cecil B. DeMille knew how to sell it. One such DeMille production advertised: "Brilliant Men; Beautiful Jazz Babies; Champagne Baths; Midnight Revels; Petting Parties in the Purple Dawn—all ending in ONE TERRIFIC SMASH CLIMAX THAT MAKES YOU GASP!"

In this climate of thinking, Griffith made *Way Down East*, a pastoral idyll, into a solid hit on the theory that there is always a place for a soundly structured picture with a valid story based on the eternal verities. He was alone in the eye of the storm, however; and Hollywood's wild parties, including a number of murders and suicides, made blacker and blacker headlines until the press began demanding that the film industry be outlawed or policed by the government, and an ever-growing number of citizens began writing their congressmen. Not until then did the producers consider changing their ways. Griffith made two trips to Washington in a vain attempt to induce William McAdoo to accept the job of film censor. Frightened over the threat of extermination, fifteen producers finally met and picked Will Hays, the Postmaster-General under Harding, to be censor of the movies. They offered Hays $450,000 as a bonus to quit his $12,000-a-year job with the government, and Hays accepted. Only a year before, following the Black Sox scandal, organized baseball had changed its image by selecting Judge Kenesaw Mountain Landis as a hard-fisted czar. Hays was no Landis, but he wrote a handbook of production ethics which the producers immediately turned into a farce. The press and public had been mollified.

In this atmosphere, Griffith's refuge was a turning back to the simple things that lie at the heart of normal human life: the adventure of the historical drama or the charm of a pastoral idyll. His pendulum ever swung between saga and poem. In 1921 Griffith chose historical drama again for his next big picture. Following *Way Down East*, he made *Dream Street*, a weak copy of *Broken Blossoms*, which he had also lifted from Burke's *Limehouse Nights*. It was another failure. He had been reading *The Two Orphans*, however, an old crock which had toured the country for years, and decided to turn this bromidic stage play into a movie. Selig had already made a movie of *The Two Orphans* during Griffith's Biograph days, but Griffith now put the Gish sisters and Joseph Schildkraut in the leads, added the Reign of Terror from the French Revolution and a sermon against Bolshevik doctrine. The picture had been well researched but proved disconnected. Griffith had been criticized for using expensive crowds of extras in *Intolerance;* now the critics were caustic about the small "mob" in *Orphans of the Storm*. (His budget had been so tight on this one that he had been forced to recruit his extras from among studio visitors.) In addition, several leading critics began referring to his perennial feminine leads as "the ever-ready Gish sisters." This picture broke even, but Griffith was strapped again. After reading the distributors' reports, Griffith released the Gish sisters from their contracts. Then Bitzer quarreled with Henrik Sardov over the latter's growing authority and issued an ultimatum to Griffith. Bitzer had been drinking heavily, and the director let him go. So ended another long relationship in the film industry.

During the filming of *Way Down East*, Griffith had received a delegation of three Russians. Voroshilov, the spokesman, asked, Would Griffith go to Russia? Deeply impressed by *The Birth of a Nation*, Lenin was offering Griffith the post of director of the Soviet film industry. The visitors returned to the Mamaroneck Studio several times until Griffith finally learned that Lenin wanted him only for propaganda films. The director said no, but an idea took shape. He had made war propaganda pictures for the American, British, and French governments, and now the Russians wanted him to glorify the Soviet Revolution. Why not propaganda pictures as a sort of peace ship for democracy? The word "propaganda" had achieved a curious stigma during World War I and the term "documentary film" had not been coined by 1920, but Griffith was already thinking in terms of the documentary when he asked himself, Why not tell the story of America?

In the same year *Orphans of the Storm* was exhibited (1922), Robert Flaherty's *Nanook of the North* was shown in New York as the bottom half of a double feature. It was a sleeper and became a smash hit; some consider it one of the ten best films of all time. Flaherty had spent twelve years filming the basic life patterns of the Eskimos. It was probably the first true documentary, as opposed to the propaganda film, that expounded and ideology although the Russians had been first to put a documentary together technically by using newsreels in Vertov's *Anniversary of the October Revolution of 1918*. Later John Grierson, the Scottish producer, coined the phrase "documentary film." Up to this time the closest thing to a documentary that the American moviegoing public had seen was the travelogue.

Griffith was impressed by Flaherty's work, observing that "you didn't need someone to write a great story for a film when the people have already written a great story with their lives." If the Soviet government could subsidize documentaries, he reasoned, why couldn't the American government do the same? He now saw the documentary film as a means of rising above the formula and sex picture competition and as an opportunity to exceed *The Birth of a Nation*. Quietly he let it be known to his old friend, William McAdoo, that D. W. Griffith would like to visit the

White House and show *Orphans of the Storm* to the President.

Orphans of the Storm opened in Boston a few days after Christmas, 1921. Shortly afterward D. W. Griffith was invited to the White House. He took along the Gish sisters and a copy of *Orphans of the Storm.* They dined with President Warren G. Harding, Vice President Charles Dawes, Attorney-General Harry Dougherty, and Ned McLean, and their wives. Afterward Griffith exhibited the picture and then attempted to open a discussion on the possibilities of the documentary film. The makings of *Tea Pot Dome* and the scandal of the naval oil leases were already in the plotting stage, however, and some of Harding's cabinet members had their minds on other things. These same people, less their wives, took the film director to the notorious house on K Street to play stud poker, a variation called Ferguson. Griffith was soon heavily in debt, but the President began playing his guest's hands until the director was bailed out. Although no stranger to sideboard whiskey, he said he was embarrassed and astonished to witness the President and his cabinet members rapidly becoming "skunk-drunk."

Griffith stayed a week in the White House, sleeping in Lincoln's bed, but no one seemed interested in documentary films except Harry Dougherty, who asked if Griffith would like to make a propaganda film for the Republican party. So the director packed his bags and went to live in a New York hotel room. He was in crisis. Upon purchasing the Mamaroneck Studio, he had formed the D. W. Griffith Corporation and sold stock to the public. His manager, Albert Grey, who was also his elder brother, was listed as vice president. The company was now in receivership, the final liquidating dividend being twelve cents per share. The high cost of operating a studio year round to make only one picture an-

nually was unrealistic—something Griffith should have learned from the reasons for the formation of United Artists. His profits from *Way Down East* were dissipated, and duns and writs had snowballed until he could no longer ignore his debts. Yet he began work on the outline of a seventy-two reel movie to be shown as a trilogy in the manner of classic novels. He also developed a stereoptic lens to give depth to the screen. Then with failing funds he backed a new theater magazine, toyed with a plan for a theater chain, and even began working on an idea for a puncture-proof tire (after an unnerving experience in the Mojave Desert).

Nobody, however, showed any desire to finance a seventy-two reel movie (although some of these same people sunk $6 million into *Ben Hur* without seeing a shooting script), and the motion picture operators lost interest in Griffith's idea for adding a third dimension to the screen when they learned that such an innovation would require an expensive switch of projectors. His ideas for thirty-five and seventy millimeter film met with the same objections. Then the two men who helped Griffith form his company to market his inventions absconded with the capital funds. When Griffith's private detectives finally located the embezzlers in an upstate New York hotel, the pair committed suicide. The money was never found.

His last idea, the embryo theater magazine, bowed out with the first issue. The theater chain idea was still a toy.

Griffith now sequestered himself in his hotel room and began sending out for bootleg whiskey. At this time, he was under heavy criticism, particularly from *Photoplay* magazine, for isolating himself from his fellow directors and for having lost the common touch. If they meant that Griffith himself did not behave as the common man did, they were right; but that was none of

141

their business. Later criticism revealed that the same critics were questioning his social values because they did not square with the fashions of the day. His films lacked sex, the new realism, and the current flip-smart humor.

The sharp and growing criticism, however, did channel Griffith's mind toward the documentary film; it was an answer to his defects as a storyteller.

Somehow, with a kind of Katzenjammer financing, he managed to mortgage every film he had made at Mamaroneck and borrow more money at usurious rates to make *One Exciting Night* and *The White Rose.* He managed to float still another loan to make *America,* a story of the American Revolution. He fled to New England with Walter Huston, whom he had known when the latter was playing in stock as "Bayonne Whipple," and wandered about, reading soldiers' diaries and studying the sites of revolutionary war battles and historic events. Stephen Vincent Benét was to do the story, but the Pulitzer Prize winner became disenchanted with Hollywood and left without finishing the script.

Although Griffith's thoughts on the documentary film were still not fully developed, some of the most beautiful photography in the documentary style that has ever been seen on the screen was contained in his fleeting vignettes of historic events and places of the American Revolution. (Bitzer returned briefly to aid on this one, then left for good.) The story was flawed, however, by Griffith's old failing: refusal to let the camera do whatever preaching he deemed necessary. In addition, the continuity was faulty and disconnected.

D. W. Griffith was $2 million in debt to the bankers when the bad news about *America* arrived from the box offices. Unfazed, he wrought a minor miracle and floated sufficient funds again to go to Germany in 1924 and make a realistic picture of the distressing economic conditions of that country. His timing and direction were off, however, as the public still flocked to the jazz age movies; and the next trend, the war movie, was just around the corner. But *America* and the German picture, *Isn't Life Wonderful,* revealed Griffith's trend toward the documentary film.

After his return to the United States, Griffith fell out with his partners at United Artists. They refused to release any more of his pictures. The fishwife bickering left him emotionally spent; so, ringed in by his creditors and doubted by his friends, he sought out Adolph Zukor and made his peace.

Zukor told the director that the name of D. W. Griffith was no longer guaranteed box office and hired Griffith as just another Paramount director without any contract clause for independent pictures. In rapid succession, Griffith made three sex movies (*Sally of the Sawdust, That Royale Girl,* and *The Sorrows of Satan*), but all turned out to be only slick copies of the work of his former pupil, Cecil B. DeMille. Such themes were beyond the ken and appetite of D. W. Griffith. (In this same year [1924], *The Birth of a Nation* was still making money. The grand old picture was booked into Chicago's Academy of Music and broke all attendance records there.)

In 1927, after an eight-year absence, Griffith returned to United Artists as a director without any special privileges. Joe Schenck was the front office now, and Griffith made three cheap silents (*Drums of Love, The Battle of the Sexes,* and *Lady of the Pavements*). He began attending stage plays to prepare himself for the new sound pictures.

Abraham Lincoln, his first sound picture, was not entirely a failure and was no worse than some initial efforts of other well-known silent directors, but Griffith was a special case. He had been too much a part of the silent picture world to make the tran-

142

sition to sound. Nevertheless, Griffith was made director of the year in 1931. Joe Schenck, however, disappointed by the box office returns, informed Griffith that Art Cinema Corporation which had been financing his pictures for release through United Artists could no longer back him. Hollywood said D. W. Griffith was through, and they were almost right. But Griffith received a sizable tax refund at this time and, with another small loan, tried the sound field again.

Taking his plot from Zola's *The Drunkard*, Griffith hired a few players, rented an old New York studio, and made *The Struggle*. It was the final irony. He again began drinking heavily when at last he had to admit that the technical aspect of sound films was beyond his competence. *The Struggle*, D. W. Griffith's last picture, opened at the Rivoli in New York, December 10, 1931, and ran for one week. It was a wretched affair, and the reviews were merciless.

In 1932, Griffith sold his stock in United Artists for $300,000. It was his last asset except for several parcels of real estate. He did a radio series on the movies, traveled in Europe, and as previously recorded, was married to Evelyn Baldwin in Louisville in 1936. The marriage was good for him but Griffith's mind had been too long in the shadow world, and he had already disappeared into his own pictures.

In 1939, after publication of the *Liberty* magazine article, Griffith was asked to return to Hollywood by Hal Roach to assist Roach in producing and directing *One Million B.C.* Griffith said that he discovered Victor Mature (Mature was already under contract to Roach when Griffith arrived on the scene) and Carole Landis—both were bit players at this time—for the leads. Griffith had once made a similar picture called *Man's Genesis* and understood the problems, but someone told him he had

been hired only for the value of his name. The old director, now hypersensitive with a touch of megalomania, disappeared for several days. When he returned, he refused to explain his absence and, according to players in the *One Million B.C.* company, ordered Roach (a former Griffith employee) off his own lot.

After the Roach affair, Griffith visited several producing companies but couldn't pass the reception desks. He became the invisible man. He phoned, wrote letters, buttonholed old friends, but received little encouragement. At this time there was a Hollywood rumor given circulation by one or two gossip columnists that there was a producers' conspiracy to bar D. W. Griffith from the film industry. It was said that the producers were concerned that if Griffith were given another chance he might run away with the motion picture business again. One critic even blamed the Russians for Griffith's demise. It was typical Hollywood sophistry. After the Roach fiasco, every producer knew that Griffith was unreliable, and unreliability and high costs are not compatible. So, if there was a cabal against D. W. Griffith, the man himself played a large role in it.

Duing World War II, Griffith frequented popular night spots where the film colony gathered, but few recognized him, and he began slipping more and more into small neighborhood bars and talking to soldiers and sailors and their dates—a nightly reenactment of Chekhov's *Dreams* wherein the derelict speaks convincingly to two soldiers in glowing terms of returning home and mending his life. Then in 1947, after bitter wrangles, he left his wife for the old Knickerbocker Hotel and semiseclusion. Mrs. Griffith sued for divorce, obtaining an interlocutory decree. On July 23, 1948, D. W. Griffith died of a cerebral hemmorrhage. The interlocutory decree had not become final, so Mrs. Griffith became

143

his legal widow. He left an estate reported at less than $80,000, but would have amounted to more if the administrators had been able to locate the banks where Griffith opened accounts, then forgot about them.

The great and near-great turned out for D. W. Griffith's funeral, including many of his old players and directors, and some who wouldn't talk to him when he was alive. There were the usual eulogies (DeMille said, "Griffith was the teacher of us all"; and Capra said, "there has been no major improvement in films since Griffith's day"), but Griffith had the last say, and Forest Lawn lost a prize catch. In his will, Griffith stipulated that he be buried in Kentucky. So the body was flown to Louisville and brought by hearse to the Griffith family plot in Mount Tabor cemetery near the village of Centerfield.

The motion picture pioneer's unmarked grave contrasted with the nearby sixteen-ton monument over his father's grave, which is fully engraved with the epic story of the old Confederate's cavalry charge in a horse and buggy. In 1950, due to the efforts of Arey Miles, a theater owner in nearby Eminence, the Screen Director's Guild sent a low, seven-foot-long marble stone bearing the Guild Medallion tastefully carved and engraved. Mary Pickford, Lillian Gish, Richard Barthelmess, and Griffith's widow

came from New York for the services. Griffith's remains were transferred to a new location, closer to his father's grave and enclosed by a corner of split rail fence from the original Griffith farm.

D. W. Griffith's grave did not become a national shrine as predicted. For years there was not even a roadside marker of the Kentucky Historical Society, and few visitors came. The quiet country churchyard, however, seems oddly appropriate for this man who left behind the motion picture as an art that belongs to the people. As Chaplin said, "Everyone who goes to the movies owes a debt to D. W. Griffith, and thus every such theater holds the spirit of D. W. Griffith." The church and cemetery are on a small rise, and looking about the green, rolling Kentucky countryside on a soft spring day, it is easy to understand why the pendulum of D. W. Griffith's mind swung between saga and poem. Not far away is the site of the first country schoolhouse Griffith briefly attended. Farther on is the pastoral idyll of Curry's Ford and the old Griffith farm, and closer at hand, the little white frame country church where he and his Sunday School class viewed the magic lantern. And only a few feet away is the grave of Colonel Jake Griffith, who left behind a legend, a pile of debts, and a little boy who loved him very much.

Carol Dempster and Neil Hamilton; *Isn't Life Wonderful*, 1924.

The story of how war demeans human beings; *Isn't Life Wonderful*, 1924.

Set in postwar Germany, this film has the quality of a documentary; *Isn't Life Wonderful*, 1924.

Griffith's mobility in moving the camera increased with the advent of the motor car.
Here he's tracking an attack in *America;* 1924.

Though *America* was not a hit, it did contain many moving and exciting battle scenes; *America,* 1924.

America is an accurate historic record of the American Revolution; *America*, 1924.

Arthur Dewey as George Washington; *America*, 1924.

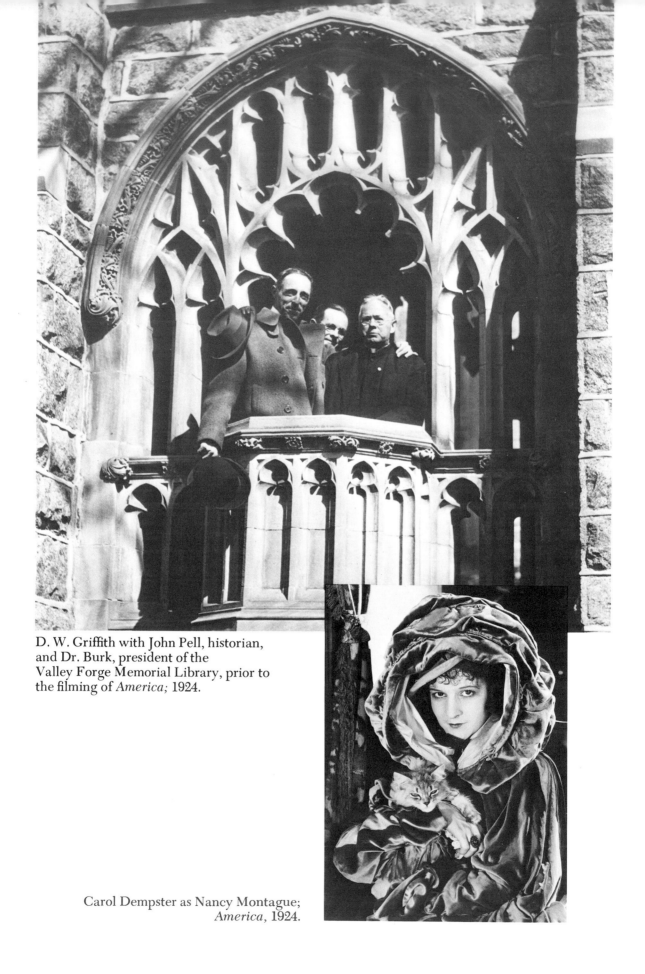

D. W. Griffith with John Pell, historian,
and Dr. Burk, president of the
Valley Forge Memorial Library, prior to
the filming of *America*; 1924.

Carol Dempster as Nancy Montague;
America, 1924.

D. W. Griffith, W. C. Fields, and Carol Dempster; *Sally of the Sawdust*, 1925.

Sally was the first major movie for W. C. Fields and marked the beginning of his star status; *Sally of the Sawdust*, 1925.

D. W. Griffith and Joseph M. Schenck, president and chairman of the board of United Artists; about 1929.

Director Marshall Neilan and Constance Talmadge, who appeared in *Intolerance*, with D. W. Griffith; about 1927.

Griffith had originally made this movie for Mutual in 1914; Jean Hersholt, Phyllis Haver, and Don Alvarado; *The Battle of the Sexes*, 1928.

Sid Grauman, Carle Laemmele, and D. W. Griffith. Grauman never captured Griffith's footprints in cement for his theater, but Griffith couldn't resist putting his initials in cement in front of his sister's home in LaGrange, Kentucky.

Walter Huston as Lincoln and Una Merkel as Ann Rutledge; *Abraham Lincoln*, 1930.

The same scene as above—this time showing Griffith directing with his crew;
Abraham Lincoln, 1930.

This film was Griffith's
first "all-talkie";
Abraham Lincoln, 1930.

D. W. Griffith with Stephen Vincent Benét,
the Pulitzer Prize winning poet who contracted to
write the script for *Abraham Lincoln*—
but quit after writing five versions; 1930.

Walter Huston was an imposing Lincoln;
Abraham Lincoln, 1930.

The tragedy of war is etched on Walter Huston's face in *Abraham Lincoln*; 1930.

A scene reminiscent of *The Birth of a Nation*—the assassination of Lincoln by Booth (Ian Keith); *Abraham Lincoln*, 1930.

On location in New York City.
The large disc is the microphone equipment
to catch sound, which was fed into
a sound truck; *The Struggle*, 1931.

Actress Lida Kane with
D. W. Griffith; about 1930.

Hal Skelly (left) in Griffith's last picture; *The Struggle*, 1931.

D. W. Griffith and neighbors
at Cox's Lake, near Griffith's
Kentucky birthplace; 1938.

D. W. Griffith's wife,
Mrs. Evelyn Baldwin Griffith,
Shirley Temple, and D. W. Griffith;
about 1935.

Albert Rogell, president of the Screen
Directors' Guild, Mary Pickford,
Mrs. D. W. Griffith, Lillian Gish,
and Richard Barthelmess at
D. W. Griffith's grave in
Mount Tabor Cemetery,
Centerfield, Kentucky; 1950.

. . . and a Backward Look

THERE ARE LAPSES, conscious and otherwise, in the autobiography of D. W. Griffith that need mending. During the showing of *The Birth of a Nation* in 1915, for example, Griffith was frequently reported as having been reared on a large Southern plantation attended by numerous Negro retainers. Actually, D. W. Griffith was born January 22, 1875, on a small dirt farm by Curry's Fork, about a mile or so from the village of Centerfield and less than ten miles from the Indiana shore—a part of Kentucky more Middlewest than South, both in culture and geography; and according to N. S. Shaler's *History of Kentucky*, there was only one slave for every five white Kentuckians in Oldham County in 1861. Also, the word "plantation" was never in general use in Kentucky. It is true, however, that the Griffith forebears held a considerable land grant at one time and there had been a large house with a few slaves, but this house was burned during the Civil War, ironically enough by Morgan's Confederate Raiders, who mistook the Griffith house for that of a "notorious" abolitionist. By 1875 many former slaves from the adjacent rich Bluegrass horse country had drifted into Oldham County to work as tenant farmers, and some of these people were the ones he reminisced about later on. Colonel Jake Griffith returned from the war and built a much smaller version (which burned in 1911) of the original house and managed to get himself elected twice to the state legislature. He was improvident, however, and D.W. was reared on hardscrabble terms.

Other apocryphal tales are probably his alleged visit to Macauley's theater with his father (a story Griffith himself circulated not a few times in Louisville, notwithstanding the fact that he was only ten when his father died) and his reputed job as a reporter under Marse Henry Watterson, famed editor of the *Louisville Courier-Journal*. Oldham County in 1880 considered the stage as sinful, and it is extremely unlikely that his mother would have permitted such an adventure. As for his being a reporter, neither the records of the *Courier-Journal* nor the files of The Filson Club, Louisville's historical society, disclose any such employment. In addition, Henry Watterson was noted for demanding strict educational levels for his staff, and Griffith had only sixth-grade schooling. His brother, Jacob, was a printer on a weekly paper at Smithfield, Kentucky, and D. W. Griffith is known to have worked in the mailroom there. Jacob later worked for the *Courier-Journal* as a printer, and D. W. Griffith is on record as having submitted theatrical notes to this newspaper for which he was paid space rates.

Griffith was bitter about certain of his boyhood experiences in a Shelby County school and dictated many pages about it, then one day suddenly cut this lengthy ref-

157

erence to a couple of paragraphs and refused to discuss the matter further. When Jeff Wylie interviewed Griffith in 1935 (some writers have confused this interview with one in 1933), he also talked to one of Griffith's schoolteachers who remembered the director as "a boy who didn't mix well with his classmates and had indifferent grades." From Griffith's own version, however, it is obvious that the Shelby County experiences had been unprintably sadistic and traumatic to a shy, sensitive boy and were certainly a pivot factor in his later isolation. He was interested in the classics at this time and was bored with the type of literature he was forced to study, an attitude that endeared him to neither teacher nor classmate. It was the custom of that day to haze any stranger who entered a country schoolroom, particularly one who didn't hunt or fish or play baseball; and Griffith admitted that he had been pampered in childhood by his adult brothers and sisters and that his classmates might well have considered him a sissy. At any rate, he never forgot the ordeal and was eloquent about it in his personal reminiscences.

Griffith's tastes in literature derived not from the New York public library as quoted by *The New York Times* but from his childhood when his sister, Mattie, read Dickens and other classics to him; from the books his father left him; and the C. T. Dearing Book Store and Ben Flexner's bookstore, both in Louisville. He often told about "a small shelf at home" that held a set of Dickens, Walt Whitman's *Leaves of Grass*, Brady's *Pictorial History of the Civil War*, an almanac, and the family Bible. (In 1939, other members of the family could not remember the Whitman book.

Griffith's mind was cast by the folk culture that stemmed from frontier Kentucky. The people had fierce clan loyalties, and any member attaining fortune immediately shared his affluence with the rest of the clan. In this respect outside critics have often misread Griffith's quick and constant generosity to his family.

At this time folk art in Kentucky was largely the art of the storyteller, and Griffith's father was a classic example. Farmer, soldier, politician: Colonel Jake was more than a mere raconteur. It is said that he never told the same story twice and that he could hold men spellbound from the country courthouse to the state legislature with tales of devotion to duty, of strength and cunning—the elemental qualities of basic folklore. The central characters of such stories inevitably became folk heroes in time, and the word-painted Hellenic murals of Colonel Jake (and many others like him), based on the adversity from which man cannot escape, were firmly impressed on young Griffith's mind. The Civil War, politics, and religion were the basic ingredients of Oldham County's folklore in the 1870's. (It should be noted that Griffith's mother was a stern-visaged woman with a large, hooked nose, who hewed strictly to an austere fundamental Methodism.)

D. W. Griffith's ties to Oldham County were the source of many of his seeming paradoxes and may account in some degree for the oscillation between poetry and violence in the making of his pictures and also for his occasional myopia and shallowness in dealing with others. And yet this "grand unsophistication," as *Photoplay* magazine called it, was somehow part of his genius: the lack of intellectual fencing that enabled him to achieve an emotional truth rather than a factual truth.

A half-century ago Oldham County was a land of great pastoral beauty, which it still is in many respects. In that day, however, the bulldozer and the beer can were happily nonexistent, and the countryside was a mosaic of rail and stone fences; quiet, crystal, purling streams and dusty lanes; gently sloping fields with wild flowers drowsing in the sun. To D. W. Griffith, this was his documentary frame of reference for *Happy Valley* and the scenes for *Way Down East* and many other pictures.

After Mrs. Griffith lost the Shelby County farm, she moved her family to Louisville in 1890, taking up residence on First Street, near Gray. Edmund Rucker, a boyhood associate and a *Courier-Journal* reporter, recalled in a 1922 interview that young Griffith promptly became infatuated with a comely young lady named Linda Lee who lived a few doors away. Linda Lee later married Cole Porter.

According to the Griffith notes, the following is the correct chronology of Griffith's early employment. Griffith's father had been a ranking Mason and now the Grand Lodge of Kentucky came to the boy's aid and was instrumental in securing his first job in Louisville—running the rope elevator and doubling as cash boy in John C. Lewis' dry goods store on Fourth Street. He was fifteen at the time and said that he "was ashamed to be seen in this job." A few weeks later a friend tipped him off to a vacancy in the C. T. Dearing Book Store at 356 South Fourth Street (now W. K. Stewart, Inc.), and Griffith was hired as a clerk. He said he liked working in a bookstore, but after a few months he was fired for reading instead of waiting on customers. He now had "experience," however, and talked Ben Flexner into hiring him as stock boy. Flexner and Staadeker's Stationery Store at 330 South Fourth Street was already quite famous in Louisville literary circles. Impromptu and informal literary roundtables were often held in the backroom of Ben Flexner's store. To these sessions came such notables as Henry Watterson, perhaps the most famed editor of his day; James Whitcomb Riley, the poet; Mary Johnson, author of *To Have and To Hold*; Adolph Clauber, who became a first-rate actor and later served as a drama critic

for *The New York Times*. (Clauber married Jane Cowl, a famous actress, and sometimes brought her to the literary sessions.) Then there was Dr. Simon Flexner, who became chief of the Rockefeller Research Institute, and many others in professional fields. As said before, these literary roundtables were impromptu and not all these people were there at once. Bernard Flexner, nicknamed Ben, was the owner and ran the place as a sideline. He was a corporation lawyer and closed the store in 1911 when he was retained by the Insull interests in Chicago.

At every such session, young Griffith brought coffee and stood on the ladder, pretending to dust books. Flexner was kind to the boy, who soon learned that discipline of the mind was teaching, not punishment, and drank in the free flow of heady ideas until his mind was spent. Sometimes Flexner allowed the boy to attend matinees in the gallery of Macauley's theater nearby, but mostly young Griffith was interested in the drama of ideas expressed in Flexner's backroom. He learned that a writer could wield fantastic power and that the stage was not necessarily sinful, and he decided to become a playwright. At this time, Walt Whitman, the father of modern poetry, still alive and one of the most controversial figures of the '90's, became a favorite with the Flexner set and especially for the young Griffith. Because of these provocative and high-minded seminars in Griffith's formative years, Biograph's director may have found the courage and vision to see the august and regal stage as a static means of producing a play and dare to move the camera to find a fluid means of expression. Regardless of that, Flexner's bookstore represented the only higher education D. W. Griffith ever received and merited more attention than he gave in his autobiography.

After D. W. Griffith went into decline, he could not resist exaggeration. His statistics on *The Birth of a Nation*, for instance, were

159

usually inflated. He preferred his press agents' version, even though the facts are astonishing enough for anyone else. Then there were his repeated claims about having innovated the close-up and fadeout. George Melies and several others had used the close-up prior to Griffith's entrance into the motion picture business (although the device was only a photographic trick at this time), and Billy Bitzer, Griffith's cameraman, claimed to have devised the fadeout. The intercutting of parallel action (such as the scene showing the husband riding to the rescue and cutting to the terrorized wife) was not an original idea with Griffith, either. His real contribution, of course, was the artistic significance and eloquence he gave to these techniques.

Griffith said he had been deeply shocked and embarrassed by the adverse publicity stemming from his handling of the black people in *The Birth of a Nation*. He thought his attitude toward the Negro had been most liberal, even though he could find nothing wrong in using a small "n" for Negro. Again, he saw nothing untoward in the sentiments expressed by the Reverend Thomas Dixon in the latter's *The Clansman* and *The Leopard's Spots*. Dixon had written that if the Negro were eliminated from social and political participation in Southern life, the South would serve as an ideal which could help redeem the rest of the nation, and recommended public support of The Clan as the best means of expediting this operation. Since it was a silent picture and Griffith had used only three pages from Dixon's work in *The Birth of a Nation*, he could claim quite accurately that he had reproduced nothing inflammatory or biased either from *The Clansman* or *The Leopard's Spots*.

D. W. Griffith freely admitted that his father held rank in the Ku Klux Klan and delighted in retelling the adventures of his father—wearing "the crested cap of cour-

age"—and his hooded mates in outwitting General George Custer's Seventh Cavalry, which was stationed at Elizabethtown, Kentucky, for the express purpose of disbanding such night riders. (Few critics, indeed, recognized that in *The Birth of a Nation* Griffith was competing with his father as a master storyteller. Here, the son was reaching into his past for his story and for the tempo and the techniques of such "folk-sayers" for emotional impact.)

Although Griffith refused to endorse the Ku Klux Klan in 1915 or thereafter, Klan leaders supported *The Birth of a Nation* and claimed the picture was responsible for a large upswing in membership. After coming under heavy criticism from nationally known clergymen, Griffith himself cut many scenes from *The Birth of a Nation*, so it would be necessary to have seen the film in its original form in order to have had any understanding of context and relevance to the charges. Those racial overtones were revived in the early '20's when Griffith became involved in a dispute with the Board of Governors of the Mamaroneck country club. When the director bought his studio on Long Island, he had lent money to the club in return for a mortgage. Irked by an action of the club governors, he reputedly threatened to sell the club to Father Divine and his black flock, and the story got into the papers.

Then there was the question of who or what was responsible for Griffith's film techniques. Sergei Eisenstein, the gifted Russian director, convinced himself that all motivation for Griffith's film techniques originated with Dickens and often went to great lengths to document this hypothesis. Eisenstein, however, was obviously unaware of Griffith's dual nature and early background. For the benefit of his mother and Oldham County pulpits, Griffith had assiduously copied and adopted Dickens as his mentor in a bizarre effort to give respectability to motion pictures as a profession. (He frequently gave public credit to Dickens for his film techniques.) It is all too true that many of his characters and stories are straight out of Dickens, but his craft of tempo and parallel action came from elsewhere. Not all critics were gulled by Griffith's deep obeisance to Dickens, as witness A. B. Walkely, writing in the *London Times* of April 26, 1922:

"Mr. Griffith found the idea (parallel action) to which he clung heroically in Dickens. . . . Mr. Griffith might have found the same practice in Dumas *père*, who cared precious little about form, but also in great artists like Tolstoy, Turgenev, and Balzac. . . . It is significant of the predominant influence of Dickens that he should be quoted as an authority for a device which is really common to fiction at large."

When shown a copy of this article in LaGrange, Griffith sniffed and said that he meant only to point out that Dickens interrupted the thread of a narrative (Griffith called it "switching off") to tell what was happening to another character not immediately related to the tale and would later bring all such excursions into a coherent whole. Then he began talking about Walt Whitman. As a highly impressionable lad, Griffith said, he had been led to tempo and parallel action in Whitman's *Leaves of Grass* by the roundtable of Flexner's bookstore, an anecdote he repeated several times in the presence of others. With his earthy ideas on sex and religion, however, Whitman had already succeeded in scandalizing rural America, and Griffith simply could not afford to openly espouse this avant-garde poet and then face Oldham County again. Dickens, however, was eminently respectable, and for Griffith to ascribe all his techniques to the popular Victorian English author was a natural ploy since he had already borrowed heavily from Dickens for character delineation and the montage of story structure.

Griffith's great contribution to the film industry lay in this mastery of parallel montage and his control of tempo for drama and suspense. (Hitchcock, Laughton, and Welles often reviewed Griffith films for aid in shoring up certain effects in their own films.) Griffith's social consciousness, however, ran no deeper than whatever action he thought was implied between the two parallel lines of rich and poor. In this respect he was following Dickens again. A carping critic may point to Edwin S. Porter's use of a crude form of parallel action in *The Great Train Robbery*, but only Griffith recognized the limitless possibilities of this device. Also, except for sound and color, there has not been any advance in basic motion picture technique since Griffith's time, and he remains the renaissance man who almost single-handedly created America's folk art—the movies. (And his star system brought them their folk heroes.) Other directors honed Griffith's techniques for qualitative effects. The next quantum jump, however, may be at hand.

Such a qualitative projection even today may still be a parlous gambit (considering the endemic itch of the Hollywood Establishment and the unblinking fact that more than a half-century has passed since the making of *The Birth of a Nation*.) But, on the other hand, when Charlie Yeager cracked the sound barrier in 1947 in a Bell X-1, you could get the same odds on when a man would stand on the moon. Too many critics have peered into Dickens and into Whitman for clues to Griffith's character and motivation when they might have fared better had they turned instead to Sherwood Anderson and his *Winesburg, Ohio*, even *Poor White*. Both Anderson and Griffith were famous for capturing life in an episodic series of moments—fleeting vignettes of rare beauty and truth—yet neither had

161

the discipline to decide on a certain effect and then immediately raid his subconscious for that particular scene. Anderson would write yards of manuscript and Griffith would shoot miles of film before each could come to his faintly outlined goal. Then, too, each listened to his father's tales of the Civil War and was obsessed by an image that kept growing with the years. And each was trapped by fame and in turn became arrogant and evasive, yet neither could bring himself to emulate Nora in Ibsen's *A Doll's House* and slam the door on the past—each was caught with his story values in one era and his techniques in another.

Many noted directors and film critics have voiced their inability to equate Griffith's one-dimensional, Victorian story posture with his great film flexibility and range. But again, any understanding of Griffith's capabilities and limitations eventually must begin with his roots. A fluid frontier philosophy was still in force in Oldham County in the 1870s which competed with the fixed, rigid Victorian credo upheld mainly by the women who clung doggedly to a stern fundamental religion to which many men paid only lip service. (A favorite bromide of the day revolved about "the lay deacon"—meaning the husband who lay under a shade tree while his wife was inside the church.) On the other hand, the unpolarized frontier philosophy was wrapped around a restless seeking of the new, the different, what was over the next hill, with great emphasis on rugged individualism; hence the rigidity of the stage was not as sacred to D. W. Griffith, as some may think, when a new medium was placed in his hands any more than the hoary English tradition of cavalry tactics was to Colonel Jake Griffith when he decided to lead a cavalry charge in a horse and buggy. Thus, when Griffith is placed properly in context with his early background, it becomes apparent why he should not be interpreted at the prime time of his career (or afterward) as a man, but rather as an idea.

There were, of course, other errors, misconceptions, and enigmas that fogged the life story of D. W. Griffith, some of which might have been cleared but for the director's own reticence on such matters. To lay this gallery of old ghosts to rest on a light note and as a bonus to car buffs, the long, sleek limousine which Dick Reynolds drove for D. W. Griffith was neither a Spanish make nor a Hispano-Suiza, as has been previously reported, but was a 540-K Mercedes and was left in Florida before Griffith's final trip to California.

In the '20s Terry Ramsaye wrote that Griffith devised the syntax for the language of the art of the motion picture. But these are writer's terms and much too limited as a measure of D.W.'s contribution. A better analogy might lie in the language of mathematics. (To Griffith himself, the word "arithmetic" meant Scrooge's bookkeeper and a diminution of spirit.) But the language of mathematics placed men on the moon, and D.W. had indeed made a quantum jump in *The Birth of a Nation.*

The great director died believing that he had failed as a writer, but in this language of unlimited horizons, he was, indeed, a great writer as well as a great artist. Perhaps his faults and aberrations were only the dross from a crucible fired too high, for D.W. was—as Josh Long, Colonel Jake's longtime friend, said—"a boy who always got there ahead of himself."

Once in China, the bearded elder of an Anhwei village asked to see my watch. The old one, wisely versed in the verities and simplicity of his life, had never seen a watch. He examined the timepiece gravely, handed it back, and said in stilted Mandarin, "It is a magnificent complication."

Somewhere between the old man and the watch lies an understanding of D. W. Griffith.

Appendix I

INVICTUS
by D. W. Griffith

EDITOR'S NOTE: The following was taken from notes narrated by D. W. Griffith for a *Liberty* magazine article.

We early movie folk were pioneers, and therefore crude, and should be remembered on such grounds. Hollywood was only a raw boom town in those days, and if new wine burst in a few bottles it should be noted that we worked incredibly long hours, and some took their fun where they found it.

We tinkered daily with the movie toy, like children making up games. Sometimes the results were comic, sometimes costly, and sometimes we pushed the industry along another inch in spite of the producers. (The ones to whom the motion picture industry today owes most are those few who strove to explore the motion picture as a medium of art.) We only wanted to make the public see. There finally came a day, however, when nobody cried, "Eureka!" any more, and there was a great stillness. The front office had won.

Hollywood today is a sterile film Detroit with emotions as standardized as automobile parts. We have moving pictures that do not move. Activity is mistaken for action; sex for love; and sound effects for suspense. If history remembers at all the people responsible for such an assembly line, it should be only for the vandalism they have wrought in a medium that could have ranked with art and literature.

There are many bad pictures and yet many people go to see them. Perhaps they haven't anything else to do. The mere lack of good art, however, does not account for such patronage. Sometimes a railroad timetable can command my interest, even if I'm not going anywhere. Therefore, if movies, even the bad ones, are witnessed in more numbers than railroad timetables, I submit that it is only because they are more artistic. At any rate, it is consoling to believe that in my

163

lifetime I have done better at entertaining the public than the gentlemen who compose railroad timetables.

We had a lot of fun in those old nickelodeon days. I remember when I paid the first star five dollars a day, and got skinned for "throwing away" $185 on one picture. Later, I played poker with a President of the United States; had a Prime Minister of England hold my coat; won an argument from George Bernard Shaw; and personally made and lost twenty-five million dollars. Pretty good for a country boy with a nose that makes me tack in a high wind.

Back around the turn of the century, however, when the movies were just getting born, I had a hole in my shoe. For ten years I led a miserable life, often shivering or sweating, always hungry. I slept in flophouses, did slob labor, and got stranded in tank towns without a cent or a friend. I was candidly a ham actor, chronically "at liberty," but it was a great apprenticeship for the work that lay ahead, and as Swinburne said, "Time remembered is grief forgotten."

Whenever I look back in memory upon the chimney pots of a small town in Indiana—my first theatrical date—I have not failed to notice that, in this particular flashback, the chimney pots always take on a rich purple, and the faces of my first troupe of actors—The Twilight Revelers—a roseate glow.

If I look back further, the lens softens even more, and that first stage in a blacksmith shop is bathed in all the primal colors of a fairy argosy.

—Interview with D. W. Griffith

James Hart
LaGrange, Kentucky

June 17, 1939

Appendix II

Chronology

1875   D. W. Griffith born on Oldham County farm near Centerfield, Kentucky (January 22).

1885   Colonel Jacob Wark Griffith, 66, D. W. Griffith's father, dies, and family moves to Shelby County farm (March 31).

1889   Mattie S. Griffith, D. W. Griffith's sister and first teacher, dies (July 21).

1890   Griffith family moves to Louisville.

1891   D. W. Griffith barnstorms southern Indiana on his first acting assignment with a troupe known as The Twilight Revelers.

1897   D. W. Griffith leaves Louisville for the New York stage.

1906   D. W. Griffith marries Linda Arvidson in May in Boston.

D. W. Griffith's sister, Annie Wheeler Griffith, dies (August 24).

D. W. Griffith plays the lead in *The Clansman* in New York.

1907   D. W. Griffith hired as a writer by The Edison Company; plays lead in *Rescued from the Eagle's Nest.*

1908   D. W. Griffith hired as an actor by the Biograph Company. In July he directs his first motion picture, *The Adventures of Dollie.*

1910   Jacob Wark Griffith, D.W.'s eldest brother, dies (December 12).

1911   D. W. Griffith and Linda Arvidson separate.

1913   Completes America's first four-reeler, *Judith of Bethulia.*

D. W. Griffith's mother moves from Louisville to LaGrange, Kentucky.

At the end of the year, he leaves Biograph and joins Majestic-Reliance (Mutual) as a director.

1915   D. W. Griffith makes *The Birth of a Nation.* Picture released February 8.

Mary P. Oglesby Griffith, 86, D. W. Griffith's mother, dies (December 11). Members of the family claimed that she never saw her son's great picture.

Griffith becomes a partner in Triangle Pictures.

1916   *Intolerance.*

1917   D. W. Griffith's first trip to Europe to aid the war effort through motion pictures.

Signs contract with Artcraft Pictures.

1919   Griffith forms United Artists with Pickford, Fairbanks, and Chaplin. *Broken Blossoms.*

1920 *Way Down East.*
1922 *Orphans of the Storm.*
1924 *America* and *Isn't Life Wonderful.*
1925 D. W. Griffith works for Paramount.
1926 D. W. Griffith rejoins United Artists.
1930 *Abraham Lincoln,* Griffith's first "talkie." Griffith leaves United Artists.
1931 D. W. Griffith's last motion picture, *The Struggle.*
       Named Director of the Year by the Motion Picture Academy of Arts and Sciences.
1934 D. W. Griffith's last sister, Virginia Ruth Griffith, dies (March 22).
1936 D. W. Griffith marries Evelyn Baldwin in Louisville, Kentucky (March 2).
       D. W. Griffith receives Special Award from Motion Picture Academy of Arts and Sciences.
1939 D. W. Griffith returns to Hollywood to work on *One Million B.C.* (June 17).
1948 D. W. Griffith dies in Los Angeles (July 23) and is buried in Mount Tabor cemetery at Centerfield, Kentucky (July 27).
1950 D. W. Griffith's remains transferred to new plot in Mount Tabor cemetery to accommodate memorial stone contributed by the Screen Directors' Guild (May 15).

Liberty

CHANIN BUILDING
122 E 42ᴺᴰ ST.
NEW YORK, N.Y.

LEXINGTON 2-9050

EDITORIAL DEPARTMENT

August 30, 1938

Mr. Jim Hart
98 Valley Rd.
Louisville, Ky.

Dear Mr. Hart:

    We may be able to use your article, D. W.
GRIFFITH LOOKS BACK ON HOLLYWOOD, if we can use Mr.
Griffith's signature instead of yours. The article
seems to be mostly by him anyway. Starting with the
fourth paragraph on page 2 until the end it is written
as if it were written by him.

    If Mr. Griffith agrees to this, we would
have to have his O.K. and signature on the first and
last pages of the manuscript.

    Will you let us know your decision?

                        Sincerely,

                        Oscar Graeve

                        OSCAR GRAEVE
                        ASSOCIATE EDITOR

OG:HW

Liberty

CHANIN BUILDING
122 E. 42ᴺᴰ ST.
NEW YORK, N.Y.

LEXINGTON 2-9050

September 2, 1938

Mr. Jim Hart
98 Valley Rd.
Louisville, Ky.

Dear Mr. Hart:

    We are very happy to learn that Mr.
D. W. Griffith will put his okay and signature
on the first and last pages of your manuscript,
D. W. GRIFFITH LOOKS BACK ON HOLLYWOOD. The
manuscript is attached.

    Will you return it to us as soon as
possible?

                        Sincerely,

                        Oscar Graeve

                        Oscar Graeve
                        Associate Editor

w
Enc: 1 ms

Collaboration between Griffith and the author on the Autobiography started after the publication of a ghost-written article in *Liberty*.

EXECUTIVE OFFICES: NEW BRUNSWICK, N. J.
CABLE ADDRESS: AFSCO, NEW YORK

ADDRESS ALL COMMUNICATIONS
ASSOCIATED FEATURES SYNDICATE

Associated Features Syndicate

TIMES BUILDING · NEW YORK, N. Y.

December 6th,1938

Mr. Jim Hart
98 Valley Road
Louisville,Ky

Dear Mr. Hart:

I hope that thenext few days mail will bring the sample Hollywood columns by David Wark Griffith.

I am contemplating a selling trip on Monday of next week which will bring me in direct contact with about fifty of the nations leading newspapers and I hope that by that time I will have received these samples together with your consent to represent you in selling this feature.

We operate the same as most of the better syndicates under which arrangement we share fifty fifty in all receipts from the sale of said feature.

I have spoken to a few publisher friends who seem to feel that a column such as we speak off,written as I know that it will should prove very saleable.

Hence I would appreciate your letter permitting us to represent you in this feature under the above terms,and we can arrange the legal details at some near later date.

Very truly yours,
ASSOCIATED FEATURES SYNDICATE INC.

Robert W. Farrell

Robert W. Farrell

RWF/ms

The idea for Griffith's doing a syndicated column was dropped when Griffith insisted on writing about world affairs rather than Hollywood. The letter from Griffith refers to a correction in the Autobiography.

Mr. Jim Hart,
Louisville, KY.

Louisville, Ky., Nov. 7th, 1938,

Dear Mr. Hart:

Enclosed please find page 109 which by mistake was omitted from my story, when submitted to you.

Am also enclosing page 71, which please substitute for the original one.

Thanking you, I am,

Respectfully,

D. W. Griffith

Per R. Speshut

Acknowledgments

To ALL THOSE kind and charming people who made this book a joy to write, the author wishes to acknowledge his indebtedness. First, to my wife and daughter who often endured the clacking of typewriter keys late at night and still kept the faith. Special thanks are also due Josef Dignan, book critic, poet, and actor, and John Maluda, the noted sculptor, for their critical opinions and years of gadfly prodding to publish the incomplete Griffith autobiography and monograph of notes.

Although this work is mainly a product of original research stemming from the 1930's, there were lately others who, because of their onetime close relationship with D. W. Griffith, offered their own collection of memorabilia of the famous film director: David Griffith Duncan, Griffith's great-nephew, and Dick Reynolds, Griffith's chauffeur, were particularly helpful, as was the late Will Oglesby, Griffith's "favorite cousin." Miss Mary Virginia Mamby, president of the Oldham County Historical Society, and W. L. Dawson, editor emeritus of *The Oldham Era*, and Gene Armstrong, the present editor, were most cooperative with their files, as was Miss Margaret M. Bridwell, a University of Louisville librarian and personal friend of D. W. Griffith.

In addition, I am warmly grateful to Don Amos for several still photographs that were hard to come by; to Bill Eisenmenger, Carl Summers, and Steve Trummer for their skill and yeoman labors in restoring old photographs; and to Paul Crane for assistance in locating scenes of Griffith's childhood. And to Clyde Townsend for his authentic and artistic water-color of Flexner & Staadeker's Book Store—D. W. Griffith's "university." Victor Mature in Hollywood was most gracious and went considerably out of his way to check the authenticity of certain Griffith anecdotes, and Dick Bertelson was effective on the Louisville end. There were many other kindnesses extended to me beyond the line of duty, including the long overtime hours of Jean Weaver and Evelyn Alsman in preparing the manuscript for the press, and the patience and encouragement under trying circumstances of the chiefs of the Touchstone Publishing Company—Don Ragsdale and Tom Ray.

PICTURE CREDITS

Pages 9–16
    All pictures are from the Collections of the Library of Congress with the following exceptions:
        page 10 (bottom right) is from the private collection of David Griffith Duncan;
        page 12 (top) is a reproduction of the watercolor by John Townsend;
        page 14 (top right) is from the private collection of David Griffith Duncan.

Pages 101-108, 117-120, 127-138, and 145-156
    All pictures are from The Museum of Modern Art/Film Stills Archive with the following exceptions:
        page 107 (top) is from the Collections of the Library of Congress;
        page 127 (center right) is from the Collections of the Library of Congress;
        page 128 (top) is from the Collections of the Library of Congress;
        page 130 (top) is from the Collections of the Library of Congress;
        page 156 (top left) is from the private collection of James Hart;
        page 156 (bottom left) is from the film archives of the Louisville, Kentucky, *Courier-Journal & Times.*

The reproductions of manuscript on pages 18 and 99 and those of the correspondence on pages 167 and 168 are from the private collection of James Hart.

This book is composed entirely in Caledonia typefaces, and the type was set by Computer Typesetting Company of Louisville, Kentucky.

Cinolith (Cincinnati, Ohio) printed this book on 70-pound *Beckett Offset* and 80-pound *Paloma* Coated Matte.

The cover material is Columbia Mills' *Colonial Lithox*, and the binding was done by American Book Company of Cincinnati, Ohio.